Bernard Stevens

Bernard Stevens and his Music

A Symposium

Compiled and Edited by
Bertha Stevens

Kahn & Averill, London
Pro/Am Music Resources Inc., White Plains, New York

First published in 1989 by Kahn & Averill
9 Harrington Road, London SW7 3ES

Copyright © 1989 by The Bernard Stevens Trust

All rights reserved

British Library Cataloguing in Publication Data
Bernard Stevens: a symposium.
1. English music, Stevens, Bernard
I. Stevens, Bertha
780'.92'4

ISBN 1-871082-03-X

First published in the United States in 1989 by Pro/Am Music Resources Inc
63 Prospect Street, White Plains, New York 10606

ISBN 0-912483-20-2

Typeset in 10/12 Plantin by Rapid Communications Limited

Printed in Great Britain by
Halstan & Co Ltd., Amersham, Bucks

Contents

Illustrations

Foreword
Robert Simpson

Bernard Stevens' music has been treated in this book by a wide range of contributors, musicians and writers of many political and philosophic complexions. This in itself is a tribute to the width of his human sympathies, which enabled his art to appeal to many different mentalities, some of whom might have been expected to be opposed to his work on account of his avowed political bent. I would not have expected this reaction from any of the contributors to this book, but their very diversity indicates the appeal, not only of his artistic achievement, but of his unmistakable humanity. There can be no doubt that in his life he suffered, with other artists, for his political views and the candour with which they were expressed. Supposedly impartial organisations characteristically exercised such prejudice with some subtlety and in such a way as to appear innocent, and Bernard was not the only sufferer. But he showed no rancour or bitterness.

He was a natural communist – that is to say he believed the widest human good to be dependent on co-operation, not on fierce strife among the ruthless and powerful for control of the planet's resources, a contest from which popular benefits might by chance appear only as spin-off. World events made him step by step aware that communism does not yet exist in the world. Hungary drove him protesting from the Communist Party in 1956, and he found no reassurance in subsequent happenings elsewhere. But his basic ideas about society remained constant.

His whole musical growth, his lifelong struggle to find ways of expressing maximum humanity, naturally and directly, showed that for him music's function was to create confidence, fellow-feeling, between composer and listener. This did not mean that he was simplistic, or bent on crude popularity; his knowledge of music was vast, and he was acutely aware that artistic work, if it is to survive, must satisfy on as many levels as possible. For this reason he made himself familiar with many kinds of music from many cultures, and was acutely conscious of the need for high craftsmanship as well as strong appeal. His feeling for the rhythmically enlivening polyphony in Rubbra's symphonies and for the Elizabethan madrigalists, as well as for the melodic and tonal refinements of Monteverdi and Purcell, was as much an intellectual as an emotional reaction.

His interest in the music of Africa and the Far East was not only an upshot of his early love of improvising – it came from his spontaneous interest in people and their needs. He was fascinated by the possibilities of ordered and memorised mass improvisation in some African music, which had natural social origins, unlike the European avant-garde's self-consciously contrived 'aleatoricism', to which he remained firmly hostile. For him written music was a necessarily difficult art, partly because it is hard to find a straight route through the bewildering array of choices confronting the twentieth-century composer. But this difficulty was for him not merely technical or intellectual. It was the terrifying problem facing any good artist – how do you get it right? And you can be worried about that only if you have something worth getting right.

Bernard's wide musical interests did not produce eclectic work. Being bent only on a true and economical expression of his own feelings for and about people, he found a music that was clearly his own. It sounds English because he was English, and it sounds human because he was human. His unaffected speech and the impression you always got from his personality of accessible warmth are reflected, now that he has gone, in the honestly searching processes of his work, sometimes a little withdrawn (as he could be in conversation), sometimes involvingly passionate (as he often tried to avoid being when talking).

The artist's main urge is to defy death by leaving behind something of himself, and something of the humanity surrounding him. There are two hopes prompting this book. One is that the species will somehow survive, and that this will be because more of its members resemble Bernard; the other is that, if it does survive, it will take a bit more notice than it has done of what he left behind him.

Acknowledgements

This symposium has been compiled with the invaluable help of John Cruft, Calum MacDonald and Roderick Swanston. Grateful thanks are also due to the many who have given their time and practical assistance in the research required for this project, to Ronald Stevenson for originally suggesting it, and to all who have so generously contributed these perceptive and human essays on Bernard Stevens and his work.

Thanks are due to:
   Alan Bousted for the copying of music examples
   Alan Jones of Fitzroy Photographic Services for his work on the illustrations
   The Dent/Trend Estate for permission to reproduce the letter from Edward Dent

Finally, to the following publishers for permission to quote from their publications:
   Bardic Edition
   Bèrben Edition
   Lengnick & Co Ltd
   Novello & Co Ltd
   Stainer & Bell Ltd
   Roberton Publications

                                                            BMS

1

Bernard Stevens, the Human Voice, and the English Tradition

Wilfrid Mellers

Britain, part of the Old World, has been in music as in many things innately conservative, though her conservatism has conservatively changed. Before the turn into the 20th century British music was in the doldrums. Indeed, whereas from the 15th to the late 17th century England had been in the vanguard musically as in other respects, she lapsed during the 18th and 19th centuries into musical unimportance, dominated by foreign models, notably Handel and Mendelssohn. The reasons for this have never been adequately explained. Though we suffered no such decline in literature and the visual arts, it seems possible that our musical blight may have some connection with the early impact on Britain of the Industrial Revolution, on which our material might was founded. It is not fortuitous that the novel, the supreme British art form of the 19th century, is the ideal medium for the exploration of psychological, social and political issues, whereas music, of its nature immediate and lyrical, is the art that lends itself least to sociological enquiry. The impulses poetically represented by Blake, Wordsworth and Keats went underground during the later 19th century, while the Empire prospered. Subterraneanly, however, their energy seethed and exploded to the surface as the old century merged into the new. This happened in the music of two composers of genius who represent opposite yet complementary poles.

Although Elgar and Delius sang an elegy on the England that had gone, they did so in a technically sophisticated, German idiom. What we now call the 'English Renaissance' was triggered off indirectly by the force of their talents; it amounted to a rediscovery, and inevitably a transformation, of the values and techniques that had typified our music in its heyday. Holst and Vaughan Williams revealed again the native English melody of folk song, rooted in the spoken language, and revived the glories of Tudor polyphony. Vaughan Williams became the crucial figure in our rebirth, because throughout his long life he sought for a reconciliation of the principles of vocal polyphony with the dramatic argument of sonata –

the critical phase of musical evolution which we had bypassed. His life's work centred on his nine symphonies; therein he solved the problem of how to create an 'English' symphony which achieved dramatic cogency while stemming from vocally conceived melodic lines. This he brought off – especially in Symphonies 3 to 6 – by way of an intuitive extension of the 16th century device of false relation: a harmonic tension between the minor and major third which sprang from a conflict between two worlds – the old monodic unity of the Middle Ages, and the Renaissance's desire for harmonic consequence and resolution.

Although Vaughan Williams became a British institution, his achievement as 'Christian agnostic' called for rare qualities of mind. He took over a centuries-old heritage of Christian faith with the musical techniques that mirrored it; at the same time he was animated by concern for the plight of modern man, as moulded by those social and political tensions – musically incarnate in sonata and symphony – which had led to the demise of the old order. For this reason Vaughan Williams had many imitators but few real successors; of them only the late Edmund Rubbra and Alan Bush, now in his eighties and still creating, are composers of comparable genus. Rubbra, too, had centred his creative life on the making of symphonies that spring from our melodic-polyphonic heritage rather than from German tradition. Unlike Vaughan Williams, he belonged to the (Roman) Church and has composed masses and motets which translate Tudor techniques into validly contemporary terms. The heart of his work lies, however, in his symphonies, in which he was 'dualistically' preoccupied with modern man's divisiveness and his need to heal breaches, while being at the same time a religious composer, 'monistically' concerned with polyphonic unity. His music creates truly symphonic drama, while being melodic in impetus, continuous in texture, consistent in figuration. Bush, though less dedicated to the English symphony, has also sought to renew the modality and polyphony of the past. As a student in Germany he early acquired a mastery of currently radical or 'advanced' techniques, which in maturity he converted to specifically English use, in an idiom as direct as it is sturdy. He too was motivated by faith: not in Christian mysticism, but in a humanist Marxism. Between them Rubbra and Bush inherit the 'Christian agnosticism' which is the heart of Vaughan Williams; the religious and social impulses, separate in the two composers, are none the less closely integrated, obverse sides of the same coin.

This approach to the music of Bernard Stevens, though circuitous, reveals the nature of his importance in British music. We don't immediately think of him as a vocal composer, and it is true that his finest work is instrumental, for orchestra or chamber ensembles. Even so, as an admirer of Rubbra and a pupil of E.J. Dent and R.O. Morris, Stevens had a thorough grounding in Tudor polyphony; and his own instrumental music, having attained maturity, resembles Rubbra's in that it generates drama from a polyphonic interweaving of lines that tend to move in vocal progression. Similarly, like Bush, Stevens has cultivated the maximum economy of linear-harmonic structure. Bush had translated Viennese serialism into an English thematicism, deriving figurations and other subsidiary elements from the main, usually diatonic, frequently modal, themes. Rubbra's continuously evolutionary flow and Bush's closely wrought thematicism are complementary manifestations of faith, religious and political. In Stevens' music the two meet. The political theme is, of course, overt throughout his life; he worked with Bush for sundry leftwing causes. The complementary religious motivation, though more covert, is manifest in his vocal music, the techniques of which are directly echoed in instrumental terms.

Among Stevens' earliest surviving works is a Mass for unaccompanied double chorus, composed in 1939 when he was twenty-three. Though the piece does not yet display the distinctive Stevens flavour, it is a beautifully written example of modal polyphony, in the tradition of Tallis and Byrd, reborn intermittently by chromatic alteration. Christian masses often reserve their finest music for the concluding section, the Agnus Dei, for this is the most ritualistically significant moment of the Latin liturgy. Stevens' Mass is no exception; its end is as moving as it is devotional. Stevens was an Anglo-Catholic in his youth; the hint of the numinous in this work suggests that the music is more than a student's exercise in an outmoded fashion. Rubbra at this time was not a Catholic but was interested in oriental religions and in Cyril Scott's brand of theosophy; later choral works of Stevens indicate that he was not immune to this aspect of religious sensibility also.

But having reached maturity, Stevens produced no more directly liturgical music. His years at Cambridge studying English literature coincided with the rediscovery of Donne, a poet obsessed with a crisis of faith; and this in turn coincided with revelatory interest in the music of Monteverdi the madrigalist, a composer nurtured in Renaissance ecclesiastical tradition while being a passionate humanist. The Italian lyricism of Monteverdi combined with 'the thew and sinew of the English language' as exemplified in Donne, to stimulate Stevens' essential creativity, and his last song was to be a setting of a poem by this passionately divided divine and libertine. Back in 1943 the *Three Donne Songs* (op.5) for high voice and piano, composed while Stevens was in the Army, were among the earliest of his published works to reveal his stature. 'Sweetest love, I do not go' is a heart-felt love song remarkable in that it sets a fairly long poem strophically, yet in continuously intense evolution. The entire piece, like so much of Vaughan Williams, stems from false relation, since both the vocal melody and the accompanying piano figurations are based on oscillations between minor and major third. The linear texture and the consistency of figuration recall Rubbra, as does the evolution of one figure into another. Tonality flows as freely as the melodic lines, though it is anchored on E flat minor, for all its modal alterations, chromatic extensions and major-minor bitonality. The sustained dialogue of vocal line with piano bass gives stability to the bittersweet passion of the ambiguous harmony; and likewise the same is true of the scherzo-like 'Go and catch a falling star'. Here the melodic cell is not that of the ambivalent third but of no less ambiguous fourths, perfect and imperfect. The traditional tritonal synonym for the devil gives aural flesh to the magical mandrake of the poem, while the sharp, glinting texture of the piano part is both airy and scary. Again the sonority depends on a bitonality in which a note a semitone away may 'stand for' the harmony note, as is evident in the odd notation in which arpeggios that sound like D flat major are (correctly) transcribed with A flats and C sharps. The necromantic quality reminds one of Busoni, a composer whom Stevens deeply admired, recognizing a temperamental affinity. The third song, 'The Good-Morrow', is the longest and the most Rubbra-like in the manner in which it grows 'morphologically', like a plant, in unbroken melodic span, in dialogue between voice and piano bass. The instrument's syncopated rhythm, pulsing like a heart-beat, is constant throughout, supporting the slowly exfoliating lyricism. Again bitonal false relations sound bittersweet, although there is no doubt that the final expansion of the melody, returning to an Aeolian F sharp, is a triumphant though severe affirmation. Here consistency and continuity of texture are an assertion of faith, no less than are similar qualities in Rubbra's music. Love between man and woman – the song is dedicated to Stevens' wife – attains a dimension beyond sex in an idiom which, despite its affiliations with Rubbra, is *sui generis*. These songs wear their forty years lightly. 'The Good-Morrow' is, by any standard, magnificent.

Another poet to whom Stevens was partial is Blake: not surprisingly, since Blake is a personal religious poet with a social conscience, prophetically aware of the human implications of the Industrial Revolution. Blake, no less than Bunyan, was an obsessive influence on Vaughan Williams, who responded to the simultaneously religious and political dimensions of both writers. Unlike Vaughan Williams, Stevens did not find in Blake an impetus for major works, and his *Two Poetical Sketches* (op.32) for women's voices and string orchestra (1961) find their texts in Blake's earliest, least characteristic and most 18th century-affiliated collection. Even so, the first of the Sketches, 'The Evening Star', is a particularly fine example of the genesis of Stevens' 'symphonic' style from vocal roots. Again melody flowers in polyphony between voices and instrumental bass; but in an orchestral, as compared with a piano, texture there is more scope for the interlacing of subsidiary parts. Again the music is Rubbra-like in its unbroken, stepwise-moving lines and in its consistent figuration. Chromatic and enharmonic fluidity is more developed than in the Donne songs, and the ambiguous tang of the harmony is now dependent mostly on oscillations between the perfect and the diminished fourth, the latter of which sounds, in equal temperament, like a major third. Such ambivalences mirror those of the poem, which describes the Evening Star's emergence through the haze of twilight. For Stevens as for Blake the star becomes a symbol of the sacred fire that defies the threat of raging wolf and glaring lion – whose thrusting dotted rhythms momentarily disturb but do not destroy the unbroken flow of quavers.

The second Sketch, 'To Autumn', is less interesting and less personal, though it displays an aspect of Stevens' music not yet referred to: his 'English' rhythmic and metrical variety, stemming from the madrigal and from Purcell. Here there are no bitonal chromatics but an unsullied (transposed) Mixolydian modality, with a middle section in straight F major, though the 'middle' does not disturb continuity. Like *The Palatine Coast* (op.21) of 1952, to poems of Montagu Slater, which Stevens described as 'Three Folkish Songs for High Voice and Piano', this sketch is very close in style to Bush in his consciously English vein. It's an inspiriting piece, though it could be by any of many post-Vaughan Williams composers, whereas 'The Evening Star' could be by no one but Stevens.

Stevens' biggest vocal work is the cantata *The Pilgrims of Hope* (op.27), for soprano and baritone soloists, chorus, strings, harp, brass and percussion (1956, revised 1968). The text, by William Morris, relates the New Jerusalem to the new world that might and ought to be achieved by socialism. Though Morris hasn't the visionary gleam of Bunyan or Blake, his vision is related to theirs and therefore implicitly to Vaughan Williams. Musically, Stevens' pastoral opening promises much, as the melody soars in cross-rhythms of $^6/_8$ and ¾ over undulating quavers. The ecstatic fervour again has affinities with Rubbra, whose presence is more darkly felt in the orchestral interlude, 'The War Machine', a very unjokey scherzo through which serpentine lines writhe over a pounding ostinato. The soprano aria 'In prison and at home', again stepwise moving but now in wavering chromatics, though not fully sustained in invention, is unmistakably vintage Stevens. Where the work lapses is in the grandiose choral movements, wherein Stevens dons the mantle of Elgar. The manner may be defended, given Stevens' level of professional competence, in a work designed as a public statement, intent on getting its message across to as wide a public as possible. For me, however, it does not carry full Elgarian conviction, and seems a lesser achievement than those passages in Stevens that burn with that visionary gleam.

This visionary gleam often occurs in two pieces that overtly compromise between religious and political motivation. *Thankgiving* (op.37) for chorus and strings (1965), and *Hymn to Light* (op.44) for chorus, organ, brass and percussion (1970) have texts by Rabindranath Tagore which are basically about spiritual illumination, though there is nothing against giving it a social-political dimension also, since no New Society worthy of the name is likely to be achieved without inner as well as outer light. The string writing of *Thanksgiving* initially generates energy from thrusting Purcellian dotted rhythms in muscular, independent polyphony; and grows cumulatively into spacious fugato on a fourth- and fifth-founded theme. Here the near-total thematicism owes something to Bush, while achieving personal identity.

In *Hymn to Light* the main fugal theme and the figurations derived from it return to Stevens' familiar alternations of major and minor thirds, and the thematically derived harmony inevitably shares in the bitonality. There's a direct affinity with the obsessive false relations in the fiercer works of Vaughan Williams, such as his Fourth and Sixth Symphonies, though Stevens' piece is less frenetic. The organ part, sinewy, without excess fat, eschews any echo of the Anglican organ loft; the choral writing, making effective play with the ambiguous thirds and with stark parallel fourths, is powerful yet within the scope of the more able parish church choir – such as Donald Hunt's at Leeds, for whom the work was written. This is more than a biographical detail; it matters that in this impressive piece the religious and social impulses, though not patently political, become one, within the traditions of an Established Church that is still a precariously living reality.

Another cantata *Et Resurrexit* (op.43), written in 1969, just before the *Hymn to Light*, compromises more openly, in that its text alternates passages from Ecclesiastes with poems of Randall Swingler. Biblical lamentation about the sorry state of fallen man is given a 20th century twist, and the procedure leads to a certain self-consciousness, even portentousness, as compared with the instinctual identity of the religious and political theme in *Hymn to Light*. Poems by Randall Swingler also serve as text for *The True Dark* (op.49, 1978), a song cycle for baritone and piano dealing in introverted private experience, without public implications except in so far as the dark night of the soul is potentially a universal experience of the psyche, as is the mind's and the world's potential for rebirth. How personal the cycle is may be indicated by the fact that Stevens composed the cycle in memory of Swingler, a close friend who had recently died, and has told us that, during the hours of creation, he was acutely conscious of the poet's presence. Certainly, the cycle is powerfully written, with all the Stevens fingerprints in evidence: oscillating thirds in the melodic line, the minor third sometimes notated as an augmented second and perhaps heard as such; a glittering Busoni-like bitonality in the two-part writing of the quick movements; syncopated rhythmic patterns throbbing against freely undulating melodies; hesitantly expectant enharmonic transitions. The relative brevity of the poems does not, however, work in the composer's best interests. Whereas in the first and third of the Donne songs the strophic verses give Stevens time and scope for his musical events morphologically to unfold, in *The True Dark* this cannot happen, and the cross-references, quotations and recapitulations, though brilliantly handled, don't quite convince as a substitute. This unease communicates itself to the vocal line, which is potently rhetorical and rewarding, as well as challenging to sing, but which, given its dramatic impetus, cannot sustain the lyrical momentum of the Donne songs. To say that the Donne songs sometimes have melodies which may be called tunes is not to demean them; on the contrary it is a pointer to Stevens' most estimable gift.

For his final song, however, Stevens returned to Donne, setting the great sonnet 'Death, be not proud' in a spacious movement lasting five minutes. The song was written in commemoration of the centenary of the birth of Teilhard de Chardin, the scientist and theologian who was also one of Rubbra's heroes, at a time (1981) when Stevens was fighting against the possibility of his own impending death; its metaphysical, though not explicitly religious connotations are thus basic. Though it is not, and given the subject hardly could be, continuously lyrical like 'The Good-Morrow', its vocal line, declamatory in its wide leaps and prancing energy, has a magnificent sweep. The piano texture begins austerely with a chord sounding fourth and fifth simultaneously, and moves into gritty parallel triads, often in false relation. The evocation of sleep as harbinger of death moves gently by step, in dialogue between voice and piano bass, with undulating figuration in middle register. The passage acts rather like a sonata second subject; and as in a sonata, positive and negative poles are held in tense balance. When, at the words 'thou art slave to fate, chance, kings and desperate men', the energetic motives return, declamatory rhetoric is more lyrically sustained, until in the final clause the melody expands progressively from second to third to fourth to fifth to sixth, giving aural incarnation to the defeat of death. The piano part sweeps through its unrelated, tonally unanchored triads over a melodic bass that falls through fourth and fifth, only to leap up an augmented octave, from G to G sharp. The voice sings the same phrase *fortissimo*, unaccompanied; and it may be relevant that the fifth and fourth (which is the fifth inverted) were traditionally God's interval, and that the octave, Milton's 'Perfect Diapason' was a symbol of the Whole. Dying, man overreaches it by a semitone, and the sound is both agony and ecstasy. The piano postlude hammers the phrase home in the bass, while falsely related triads thrust upwards in the right hand. The final chord repeats the fourth-fifth complex from which the work had started, a third higher.

It may be my predilection that leads me to think that Stevens' finest vocal music is that closest to his personal rather than public experience. Yet the Donne songs, the first of the *Poetical Sketches*, the *Hymn to Light* and perhaps *The Pilgrims of Hope* are not only Stevens' most personal vocal works but also those that communicate most directly as well as deeply. Their vocal idiom approximates to that of his most 'abstract' instrumental works, such as the Piano Variations of 1941, the Piano Trio of 1942, the string quartet Variations of 1949, the Piano Sonata of 1954, the String Quartet of 1962, and the Second Symphony of 1964. These works contain Stevens' quintessence, I believe; this is not to deny that their 'message' is inseparable from that of the vocal pieces. The problem of the English symphony, as outlined in the introductory paragraphs to this essay, remains no less fundamental than the crucial operatic theme which, through the work of Britten and Tippett, has dominated our music since the Second World War. As the years roll on I suspect that we will see or rather hear how Stevens provides an essential link between the symphonic achievement of Vaughan Williams and Rubbra and the currently evolving work of Robert Simpson, and his stature is commensurate with theirs.

Press photo, 1946 *Daily Express Victory Symphony Competition*
Prizewinner.

2
The Choral Works
Alan Bush

In 1946 Bernard Stevens became suddenly famous; he won the composition competition organised by the *Daily Express* for an orchestral work which he entitled *Symphony of Liberation*. The work's three movements were given the titles 'Enslavement – Resistance – Liberation'. The liberation celebrated therein was the defeat of Hitler fascism. I well remember the first public performance of that work in the Royal Albert Hall.

Up to that time British composers of rank who expressed progressive social or political ideas in their works could be counted on the fingers of one hand. Rutland Boughton was the first British musician of rank to join the British Communist Party, in 1924; he visited the Soviet Union in 1925, and founded the London Labour Choral Union, a federation of working-class choirs, in that year. Boughton never included political subjects in any of his ten operas; in his choral works, however, to texts by Edward Carpenter and Walt Whitman, he introduced subjects outside the usual blameless conventionality acceptable to our British choral societies.

In such conditions of British musical life the appearance of a *Symphony of Liberation* was an event of outstanding artistic and social significance; moreover it introduced to the general musical public a creative personality of high distinction.

Shortly after the performance of this symphony Stevens wrote the first of his fifteen choral works, *One Day*, to a poem by David Martin. It opens with the words:

> One day the young will die no more
> Before their youth is riper.

The four verses are all set to grave melodic lines with the phrase structure A^1 A^2 B, though in each verse subtle variations of detail in the note-values and intervals are introduced where required by the demands of the text. A broad introduction on the piano, and substantial bridge passages between the verses, involve modulations and introduce interesting and expressive contrapuntal

developments. *One Day* is indeed a noble choral work, effective
with a mixed choir of either moderate or substantial size.

The fifteen choral works include two powerful working-class
marching songs, *The Password* and *Workers of the World, Unite!*,
and also *Colliers' Song*, in which the harsh conditions of coal-getting
with 'pain, twisting and struggling' form the subject. All but one,
Take all of man, are accompanied; three by orchestra, three by
string orchestra, one by string quartet and piano, and seven by
piano alone. In ten of these works the texts were chosen from
English and Irish poets, of whom all except William Blake and
William Morris were of the twentieth century; the poet most frequently chosen was Randall Swingler. The words of *Et Resurrexit*
are from *Ecclesiastes* and Swingler, and those of *Thanksgiving* and
Hymn to Light are by Rabindranath Tagore.

The text of *The Password* by Montague Slater refers to the scene
of working-class struggle, Madison Square, New York. The basic
tonality is E. Verses 1, 2 and 3 approximate to the Dorian mode
on E, and verses 4 and 5 to the Mixolydian mode, also on E. But

raised leading-notes and transient modulations to D and G negate a clearly modal idiom, and produce a most original scale from which the melodic intervals and harmonic vocabulary are derived. Quick march-time is the composer's tempo indication. In the two-part piano accompaniment incessant crotchet movement in the bass and equally incessant imitative counterpoint in the treble, whose thematic material is quite independent of the vocal line, result in a choral piece of 39 bars of fierce urgency and pronounced originality.

Not *Quick march-time* but *Allegro deciso* is the tempo indication given to the choral song *Workers of the World, Unite!* This world-famous rallying cry, with which Marx and Engels closed their Manifesto of the Communist Party in 1848, is the sentence with which the text of Stevens' most direct song of workers' struggle begins and ends. The writer of the text is unknown. It is a short concert-piece of 52 bars. There are three verses, two of four lines, one of three lines; a two-bar introduction on the piano recurs between the second and third verses. The basic tonality is F major; D minor, A minor, C minor and G Minor all make their appearance. The imaginative choice of unequal lengths in the verse structure, and the five tonalities deployed, are precisely the features necessary to produce freshness in a piece of music which might otherwise sound square and repetitive. As it is, it carries the listener determinedly forward.

The last of the shorter works is *Running to Paradise*, to words by W.B. Yeats. It is a part-song for S.A.T.B. and piano. The

strange text expresses, though in an obscure fashion, the belief
that there will be established on earth a Paradise, a state of human
life in which 'a king is but as the beggar'. The poet, running to
Paradise, sings:

> Yet never have I lit on a friend
> To take my fancy like the wind
> That nobody can buy or bind.

The basic tonality is the Aeolian mode on E, but already in the
first verse there is a modulation to G Phrygian. The vocal line sets
the words admirably. The basic rhythmn is a quick ⁶/₈, but the
second and third verses introduce rhythmic variations. The ending,
which rejoices in the beggary of the king, is set triumphantly in the
Lydian mode on E. It is a most striking composition.

   Six of the choral works are of substantial length. *The Harvest of
Peace* (op. 19) is a cantata to words by Swingler, for soprano and
bass soloists, speaker and chorus, with string orchestra or string
quartet and piano. The first movement, 'Rachel mourning for her
Children', is a tragic lament; Rachel's children are the thousands
of innocent children murdered or gravely injured by the aerial
bombardments of the Second World War. 'The Wind's Song',
a wild scherzo ranging from *pianissimo* to *fortissimo*, presents 'a
wind like a rocket, like a spout, a wind to find you out', that is,
if you do nothing about the state of the world. The title of the
last movement, 'The Re-awakened Forest', comes from the last
line the chorus sing: 'The green peace, the re-awakened forest of
Man's love'. The soprano soloist starts the movement with:

> Our hope to certain morning grows
> Wherever man looks up and sees
> His realm expanding like the day's
> Unfettered trade-route through the skies.

These lines also form half of the text of the third movement
of *The Turning World*, written in 1971, nineteen years after *The
Harvest of Peace*. In the second setting the vocal line and harmonic
progressions are exactly the same as before, but their presentations
are strikingly different in the general orchestral texture, with
different note-values built into the bass and middle parts. The
expressive contrasts between these two presentations, each equally
convincing, provide one of many evidences of the composer's
imaginative and emotional range.

The roseate prospect of this text ignores the threat of the neutron bomb with its devastating potential, a hundred times greater than that of the atomic bombs dropped on Hiroshima and Nagasaki. 'Our hope' is dim indeed unless more resolute action is taken by the peoples in all countries of the world against the present threatening world situation.

At this point some exposition is necessary of the harmonic vocabulary employed in many of Stevens' developed choral works, and his particular use of it, which is a highly original feature of his creations. Striking examples of it occur in *The Harvest of Peace* and *The Turning World* just mentioned.

The third movement of *The Harvest of Peace* begins with an introduction of eight bars in which the chord of B flat gradually appears, first in a single line, then in two and finally in six voice parts, leading to the first line of a solo song in G major in slow $\frac{4}{4}$ time. This first verse of the solo song consists of eight beats of G major, eight of E major, eight of C sharp major and eight of B flat major; then these harmonic progressions are exactly repeated with the same number of beats, leading finally to eight beats of the G major tonic. The positions of the chords vary as follows:

G major   1st inversion
E major   2nd inversion

C sharp major	root position
B flat major	1st inversion
G major	2nd inversion
E major	root position
C sharp major	1st inversion
B flat major	2nd inversion
G major	root position

The bass part has thus a continuous rise from B to G of major or minor seconds with, at one point, an enharmonic change from E sharp to F natural. The voice part during the first harmonic progression of G, E, C sharp and B flat includes all the twelve semitones; in the second section of eight bars its melodic line is developed from what has come before, without any exact repetition, and sometimes by inversion of intervals. This description indicates the composer's originality and highly developed technical ability, as does his remarkable precision in the treatment of unessential notes in the vocal and instrumental parts, where all are resolved in classical style.

The Pilgrims of Hope (op. 27), a cantata for soprano and baritone soloists, chorus and orchestra, is the most important of the five larger choral works; the text is by William Morris. It consists of five movements and an epilogue:

1. 'The Message of the March Wind' for baritone and orchestra
2. 'How near to the Goal are we now?' for chorus and orchestra
3. 'The War Machine' for orchestra alone
4. 'In Prison and at Home' for soprano and orchestra
5. 'What are these Tales of Old Time?' for chorus and orchestra
6. Epilogue: 'O Earth, Look on thy Lovers' for soprano and baritone, chorus and orchestra

This work was composed in 1956 and revised twelve years later; the musical forces involved are interestingly varied, and only in the Epilogue are all employed together.

The vocal lines in all Stevens' works are very straightforward. In the first movement of *The Pilgrims of Hope* the baritone solo part does not include one single chromatic, augmented, or diminished interval. The rise and fall in pitch nearly always reflect the natural intonation of the accented and unaccented syllables of the poem. There are two exceptions to this: at one point the word 'people' is set with its unaccented second syllable rising, and at another point the word 'seeketh' is set with its second syllable unduly lengthened. In 128 bars of music these defects are indeed few.

Imitation has long proved an irresistible temptation to English choral composrs, even though it results in the simultaneous singing of two or more different syllables, making whole paragraphs of the text unintelligible in performance. As a rarely exceptional occurrence, in the second and fifth movements of *The Pilgrims of Hope* some few lines of the text are set with imitations, but this is done in such a way as to avoid any confusion in the verbal effect, the chief melodic line being sung in octaves by the sopranos and tenors, with only fragmentary imitations in the alto and bass parts. Except at such points, the syllables of the text are set quite straightforwardly, without imitations and with appropriate note-values and variations in pitch. Here follows an example from the baritone solo part, where such confusion could be more easily overcome by a solo singer than in the choral section, but where the composer has taken great trouble to provide notes and note-values perfectly fitted to the verbal requirements of the text.

In this passage the composer has reverted to the extraordinary harmonic structure which is such a striking feature of *The Harvest of Peace* and *The Turning World*, mentioned previously.

The third movement, 'The War Machine', is a ferocious march for orchestra alone. Heard at first in the distance *pianissimo*, it comes gradually nearer, reaching *fortissimo* 61 bars later; the melodic line is developed exclusively from major and minor seconds, with an occasional leap upwards of a perfect fourth. After six bars of *fortissimo* the dynamic falls to *piano*, but the excitement is maintained by the introduction of continuous quaver triplets. A second *crescendo* leads to the *fortissimo* climax, which is sustained for 21 bars; 28 bars of recapitulation bring the movement to a violent conclusion.

In the *adagio* fourth movement, 'In Prison and at Home', the hero's wife sings of her loneliness.

The desolate poem is set to finely moulded melodic lines with a continuous four-part accompaniment, scarcely a rest interrupting its flow. In the first bar an inverted major seventh chord leads to the slow-moving introduction of eight bars, which precedes the first verse in an uneasy G minor tonality. In this whole movement there is not one single consonant chord except at the beginning of the final phrase of the 17 bar coda, which, however, ends on the D minor chord with a major seventh. This is a most impressive movement, in which the tragic text receives heartrending and at times impassioned expression. It demands much from the singer, even though the upward compass of the part does not extend beyond A in alt.

A bridge passage of two bars introduces the shorter fifth movement, for chorus and orchestra. The harmonic structure of this movement recalls that of *The Harvest of Peace* and foreshadows that of *The Turning World*; regular phrase lengths of four bars again appear, except that in one case a five-bar phrase occurs. The five phrases of the first verse are built on C major, A major, F sharp major, A major and again C major. After an orchestral bridge passage the four phrases of the second verse present C sharp minor, B flat minor, G minor and E flat major; their phrase lengths vary with five, four, six and four bars respectively. The forceful choral writing, often marked *fortissimo*, is effectively varied by the choice of voices for the various phrases. In the first verse full chorus, male voices, female voices, and again full chorus, succeed one another; in the second verse they appear in a different order. In the short third and last section only is full chorus used. It is here that one of the passages of imitation occurs, and with the *più mosso* indication it provides an additional force and excitement to the rather enigmatic couplet:

> That never again, like ours,
> May be manhood spoilt and blurred.

The Epilogue follows upon the fifth movement without a break. The basic tempo is a broad *andante* but, starting quietly, a fierce *accelerando* to twice the speed brings the climax, a cry of thankfulness that such a habitation as the earth exists, where lovers could know and appreciate its richness, and yet choose a life of struggle for a way of living, such that:

> Man to man may hearken
> And the Earth her increase yield.

With *The Pilgrims of Hope* Stevens created one of the most notable British choral works written since the Second World War.

There now remain to be considered *Two Poetical Sketches*

(Blake), *Thanksgiving* (Tagore), *Et Resurrexit* (Ecclesiastes and Swingler) and *Hymn to Light* (Tagore). In the first two works (1961 and 1965) and in part of the third (1969) Stevens chose texts which are markedly different from any others set by him.

The *Two Poetical Sketches* (op.32) for women's voices and string orchestra or piano, bear the titles 'To the Evening Star' and 'To Autumn'. In the first song murmurous quavers flow gently and uninterruptedly for 64 bars. Then references in the poem by Blake to 'the raging wolf and the glaring lion' break into this quiet flow, but only for ten bars, after which it is resumed. In this first song the exquisite poem is set to a very smooth vocal line, in which major and minor seconds predominate, with occasional rising perfect fourths; at one single point a leap upwards of a minor sixth. The chorus part rarely exceeds two-part writing; passages in three parts occur in only 19 of the movement's 64 bars. The harmonic progressions are developed from major thirds and perfect fourths in C major and D flat major chords respectively. This is a most striking piece of music. The second song is an *allegro*. Here rising sixths in the voice parts are an important feature of the opening phrase, and recur in a later stanza. The key is the Mixolydian mode on F with a middle section in the same mode on C; there are not in either the vocal or the orchestral parts any notes outside the diatonic notes of these two modes. In these *Two Poetical Sketches* the composer employs technical command and creative originality of a high order; the undeviating stylistic consistency shows mastery and very delicate aural sensibility. The vocal demands are moderate. The first soprano part never rises beyond G; the whole range of dynamic from *pianississimo* to *fortissimo* is not excessive; one phrase requires from the first sopranos *ppp* as high as G flat, but this occurs on the syllable 'Ah', which facilitates its performance considerably. This work deserves the attention of good female choirs throughout Britain.

Thanksgiving (op.37), a motet for mixed chorus and string orchestra (or organ) was written for Denys Darlow and the Tilford Bach Choir. It could hardly be more opposite in every feature. The text by Tagore is forceful, and in fact imprecatory. The poem begins:

> Those who walk on the path of pride,
> Crushing the lowly life under their tread,
> Covering the tender green of the earth

With their footprints in blood,
Let them rejoice and thank thee, O Lord,
For the day is theirs.

But the poem foresees their eventual downfall; it ends:

O sun,
Rise upon the bleeding hearts
Blossoming in flowers of the morning,
And the torchlight revelry of pride
Shrunken, shrunken, shrunken to ashes.

The music is appropriately violent. The rising and falling fourths and semitones of the two voice-part opening sound rough and fierce, even on the organ. The ending of the chorus part, 'Shrunken, shrunken, shrunken to ashes', is set *forte*, rising to *fortississimo*, and is followed by two bars on orchestra (or organ) which rise to an unusually spaced chord of E without either major or minor third, a striking feature since G sharp is a prominent note in all the preceding four bars; its bareness well expresses the composer's last word of warning to 'those who walk on the path of pride, crushing the lowly under their tread'. On a Sunday morning this work would make an invigorating change from the soothing complacency of most Anglican anthems.

Et Resurrexit (op.43), a cantata for alto and tenor soloists, mixed chorus and orchestra, was also commissioned by the Tilford Bach Society, with the assistance of Mr Peter Morrison. It is dedicated 'In Memoriam Randall Swingler', and is in three movements, to words from *Ecclesiastes* and Swingler, with an orchestral interlude after the second movement. The harmonic vocabulary is more elaborate than in previous works; nevertheless its basic method of progress follows from that underlying the earlier compositions. The first movement, 'Roll away the heavy stone', for alto, chorus and orchestra, begins and ends on the G minor chord. In the orchestral introduction the chordal succession G minor – B major – F major – C sharp minor appears in various phrase lengths.

Similarly, after the entry of the soloist, it recurs again three times. With a threatening excerpt from *Ecclesiastes* the chorus breaks in on the song, but the chordal succession reappears. An extraordinary three-bar passage follows, where the bass of the fourth bar's C sharp minor harmony overlaps the G minor chord, after which an orchestral bridge-passage, starting *fortissimo* and sinking to *mezzopiano*, modulates to *pianissimo* B minor. On a pedal B *Ecclesiastes* is heard again.

> That which hath been
> Is that which shall be
> And that which hath been done
> Is that which shall be done
> And there is no new thing
> Under the sun.

The bass part finds its way back to G with alternating G minor and B major chords, and the movement closes *pianississimo*. Technically this first movement is most skilfully developed. During the first 16 bars of its orchestral introduction phrases in two- and three-part counterpoint alternate with four-part harmony; in it many of the thematic details in the different voice parts are developed from the contrapuntal phrases. The tempo is *andante*, but agitation becomes paramount in the second phrase of 16 bars, with double-dotted quaver and demisemiquaver note values.

The second movement, 'The dying eyes', for tenor and chorus with orchestra, also begins *andante*, but with a slightly faster metronomic indication: its tempi vary a great deal between crochet = 60 and crochet = 168. No one tonality is maintained for long; the first stanza begins and ends in E flat major. An orchestral interlude, more than half the length of the orchestral opening, leads to the first major climax with the emphatic choral statement:

> This, this, this, this
> The true resurrection is!

The section ends on an E flat major chord. The tenor solo phrases which follow immediately are developed exclusively from rising minor thirds and semitones, and the two-part orchestral accompaniment likewise. Two new harmonic motifs then appear and take precedence over all else: a major triad leading to a minor triad in first inversion, and a minor triad leading to a major triad in first inversion:

The poem ends positively:

> I saw all the living
> That walk under the sun
> And they were with the youth!

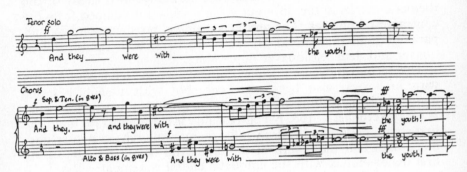

There follows immediately an orchestral interlude: Scherzo, as it
is designated in the score:

It is a rapid ⁹/₈ *Allegro*, 99 bars in length. From the fifth bar
continuous movement of nine quavers in the bar is maintained
until the final cadence is reached. Beginning *fortissimo*, the dynamic
indications *mf subito* or *mp subito* rising to *fortissimo* occur seven

times, to *fortississimo* twice. It is a tumultuous piece of music in two sections: the first a four-part fugue; the second basicly in two 'voices', one of which, however, is thickened sometimes in close triadic first inversions, elsewhere in widely extended triads or chords of the seventh. There then occurs an interruption which recalls the orchestral interlude-scherzo, with its violent contrasts and *accelerandi*. This leads finally to Swingler's 'Gloria', with which the cantata ends.

In 16 bars of orchestral introduction Stevens unifies the new 'Gloria' motif with a passage in which the harmonies of the 'Resurrexit', altered to successions of major triads only, are combined with a new flowing counter-melody, developed from the orchestral opening bars of the cantata. This final section, as

eloquent as it is effortlessly integrated, ends with acclamation of the world's wonders:

> Glory then, glory to the young leaf!
> Glory, no less, to winter's tender grief
> Which uncovers and waters the hidden roots

Of longing and of love
And at last returns earth's dew-fresh daughter
From her Demetrian womb
To her new-found, majestic, paternal Sun.
Glory! Glory!

The last work to be considered is *Hymn to Light* (op. 44), an anthem for chorus, organ, brass and percussion. The text, taken from *Fruit Gathering* by Rabindranath Tagore, imparts something of the composer's joyous acceptance of life, already expressed in *Et Resurrexit*. But it is not spring with its renewal of life or even the glorious sun which is the subject of this poem, but light itself. 'Night is pierced through' and 'cut in twain the tangle of doubt and feeble desires'. At the close 'Death dies in a burst of splendour'. In the music the intervals of the major and minor third are predominant in both melody and harmony; two major thirds add up to an augmented triad, so that this chord occurs frequently. In the tonality E and C predominate, but the triumphant ending takes a sudden turn to E flat major. By design or coincidence the motif of the notes C, E flat and E natural is a precise transposition of the notes C sharp, E natural and F, with which the prelude opens and from which the first 20 bars of the main *Allegro* are developed in the orchestral part. In this remarkable work, the last but one choral work to be completed by Stevens, the principle of thematic development is applied consistently, a technical feature which appears in his choral works for the first and only time and rarely elsewhere except in his instrumental fugues.

This survey and assessment of the choral works of Stevens may come as a surprise to some readers, who will be familiar with Britten's *War Requiem* and Tippett's *Child of our Time*, both of which have enjoyed well-deserved success. Regrettably they may have heard little of the music of Bernard Stevens, let alone have experience of his major choral work, *The Pilgrims of Hope*, with its text of such high artistic quality and its musical setting so fully equal to such a searching demand.

Accompanying the Workers' Music Association Choir at the
World Youth Festival. Prague 1947.

Giving a lecture at the 2nd International Congress of Composers in
conjunction with the Prague Spring Festival of 1948.

3
The Violin and Cello Concertos
Stephen Johnson

Bernard Stevens wrote two concertos for solo string instrument and orchestra: the Violin Concerto of 1942-3 and the Cello Concerto of 1951-2. The Violin Concerto was the first major orchestral work Stevens composed after leaving the Royal College of Music; he had been toying with the idea of writing a concerto for this instrument for several years, but it was only when Max Rostal saw the sketches and expressed interest that he began to work on it in earnest. At the time Stevens was still in the Army and much of the concerto was apparently written during intervals in guard duty; nevertheless, despite physical exhaustion and the continual rowdiness of the other soldiers in the barracks, Stevens managed to complete the work within six months. It seems that the urge to compose was too strong to be denied:

> I found it much easier to concentrate on creative work at that time, in [spite of] what seemed like impossible circumstances . . . The importance of creative work in wartime, personally as well as collectively . . . was very great, so that I was able to overcome purely physical problems.

But it wasn't only the 'purely physical problems' that had to be overcome; there were artistic conflicts that demanded resolution. For some time Stevens had been fascinated by the music of the Jewish composer Ernest Bloch. The dark intensity and sustained romantic lyricism of Bloch's music had been a strong influence on the style of some of Stevens' earlier works, and yet he felt that it lacked what he called 'inner rhythmic life', a quality which he had observed in the vigorously contrapuntal music of his older contemporary, Edmund Rubbra. In the Violin Concerto Stevens sought to bring together the lyricism of Bloch and the contrapuntal vitality of Rubbra. It seems, however, that he could not be satisfied with a simple juxtaposition of the two styles; rather, the lyrical and contrapuntal elements had to be united in a kind of 'melodic polyphony'. This is how the work opens:

Working in his Belsize Park studio – with assistant 'Monteverdi'.

Ex 1 Andante (♩=92)

A sinuous chromatic melody is presented by the violas, and re-stated, at the interval of a minor sixth, by the second and subsequently the first violins. As in a number of the solo instrumental works of J.S. Bach, this 'melody' actually comprises two independent voices moving in counterpoint: what we have here is, in effect, a combination of two chromatic scales, one rising from the G below middle C, the other falling from G an octave above. These lines cross at the C sharp in bar 4 and then continue, the rising line becoming the lower voice of the theme in bar 5, the falling line continuing as the cellos' descending countersubject in bars 5 to 9. Both the ascending and descending countersubjects are clearly derived from the outline of the violas' theme, but Stevens makes sure this relationship is understood when the music reaches its first climax at bar 21:

Despite the transposition of the lower voice up a minor third (first trombone), the two superimposed chromatic scales are still strongly suggestive of the contours of the opening viola melody.

Interestingly enough, this splendidly versatile theme had occurred to Stevens long before he began work on the Violin Concerto. It first appears in a quasi-fugal *Toccata*, an early piano piece that he wrote while studying at Cambridge (in ⁴/₄ rather than ⁶/₄ and with a slightly different rhythm in bar 2) though, as Stevens himself admitted, the new continuation is a considerable improvement on the original, which contained a rather over-intricate countersubject (see p.45); moreover there is an important addition to the texture: a gently pulsating pedal G on timpani, horns, second bassoon and basses. This fulfils two functions: firstly, it defines the ⁶/₄ beat and thus makes the syncopations of the countersubjects (the 'inner rhythmic life') more effective; secondly, it provides a tonal 'anchor', ensuring that the chromaticisms of the upper parts can be heard to relate to the fundamental G major-minor. For Stevens it was the 'tonal possibilities of chromatic themes' that were of particular interest; non-tonal, or to use Schoenberg's preferred term, 'pan-tonal' serialism seemed to him barren and lifeless in comparison.

The above analysis, brief though it is, should give some idea of the intensiveness of the writing in the opening *ritornello*: everything in the first 30 bars of the movement relates directly to the basic material of Ex.1, and the linear combination of two voices in the opening theme means that it is suitable for both melodic and contrapuntal developments. Nevertheless, with the entry of the soloist in bar 31, the line of demarcation soon becomes apparent. Lyrical elaboration is, on the whole, left to the violin, while true polyphony – the combination of equal and independent voices – occurs only in the orchestral passages and in the unaccompanied cadenza where the influence of Bach's solo instrumental style is particularly apparent. When soloist and orchestra play together it is the violin who leads the argument, no matter how intricate the accompaniment. Note how at bar 37 the violin extracts a figure from the final bar of the opening theme (marked x in Ex.1) and meditates on it high above the orchestra: the cellos and basses are allowed to participate, but their role is purely imitative – they merely 'echo' the violin figures:

This trend continues in the other two movements: the beautiful canonic writing at Fig.13 in the *Adagio* ceases as soon as the soloist enters; even so, Stevens has considerably enriched his musical language as a result of his labours in the first movement. The occasional suggestion of constructivism, particularly with regard to the manipulation of leading motives, does not detract from the sense of new-found confidence that permeates the work.

The first performance of the Violin Concerto was highly successful, and it was played several times during the immediate post-war period. Nevertheless, despite widespread critical recognition of his achievements in this work, Stevens began to find what he called the 'over-intense, rarified world' of the concerto a little difficult to live in. Subsequent compositions show a gradual return to a more relaxed and direct lyricism. In the years that followed, not only his musical style, but also his personal circumstances changed. Just before he began work on the Cello Concerto, Stevens bought a house in the Essex countryside, seeking an environment more conducive to composition; in addition his wife, Bertha, was expecting their first child. These factors may have contributed to the prevailing mood of the concerto, but they do not account for the extraordinary inventiveness and mastery in the handling of musical resources that Stevens shows here.

The opening paragraph of the concerto is worth quoting in full:

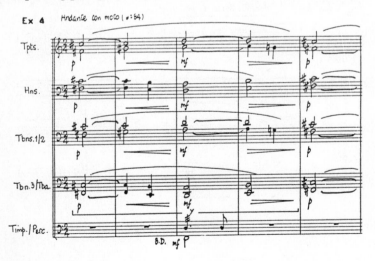

At first the music seems to be rotating around the key of F sharp minor, but the gentle insistence of the timpani (supported by the bass drum) eventually brings about a cadence in D, which turns out to be the home key of the work. The cello then enters with a long, almost vocal melody, dominated by the interval of the perfect fourth:

Note the appearance of the bass figure y from Ex.4 (in inversion); it recurs in various guises throughout the movement:

As the movement nears its end it is only just recognisable:

Early on, in a slightly extended form it gives rise to the cello's version of the second subject:

As the movement progresses and the mood darkens, the pure fourths of Ex.5 are gradually replaced by the interval of the tritone. By the time we reach the climax of the movement, Ex.5 looks like this:

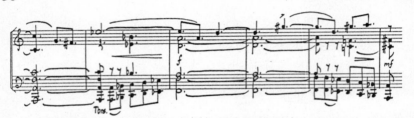

The cellist then takes up Ex.9 embellishing it with a series of harsh semitonal appogiaturas:

The recapitulation is highly condensed and the movement seems almost deliberately foreshortened. In the final bars a reminder of the second subject (Ex.6c) rises and falls darkly in the cellos and basses, while the solo cello spits out the rapid appogiaturas of Ex.10. The movement ends in a troubled D; resolution and consolidation are temporarily deferred.

The central movement is a magnificent *Chaconne*. Here Stevens confronts the tensions that disturbed the serenity of the first movement's opening *Andante*. Note that in the first movement the more impassioned versions of the cello's original theme (Ex.9 and 10) were in F sharp, the 'false tonic' of Ex.4; this now becomes the home key of the slow movement, though at first F sharp is heard as the bass of a stridently elaborated diminished seventh.

There are two brief, recitative-like introductions, in which the cello gradually turns away the wrath of Ex. 11, bringing about a quiet resolution in F sharp minor. Trombones now present the harmonic framework of the Chaconne theme as the accompaniment to a series of piognant three-bar phrases on first violins and cellos:

Ex 12

a)

b) Trombones continue, same rhythm

The trombone chords recall the original seventh (Ex.11), but the tension of this dissonance is somewhat reduced as each note is harmonised by a simple minor triad, and thus the process of resolution begins. As the Chaconne proceeds, it mirrors the tendencies of the opening movement: the *Andante* becomes more restless and impassioned as it progresses; here the tension slowly unwinds. The constant, circular motion generated by this continuous variation structure gives the music a contemplative quality: no matter how intense the foreground activity, one is always aware of a firm background – an inner calm. Gradually this sense of peace spreads throughout the music: the painful expressions of Exs. 11 and 12 are soothed into stillness. In the final variation only the regular rotation of Ex.12 is left, along with a calmer version of the violin and cello theme (cor anglais, *mezzopiano*) and a ghostly echo of the original dissonant seventh, now absorbed into the fundamental harmony:

Ex 13

D major is briskly resumed at the start of the *Finale*, and although there is a great deal of oscillation between the pitches of F sharp, D and B flat (cf. Ex.4) the tonic is never seriously in doubt. For the most part, the music is jubilant and dance-like; only once, just before the cadenza, is the brightness dimmed by a reminiscence of things past. A figure resembling Ex.10 is taken up by the cello, *meno mosso*, over a simple accompaniment of bassoons and off-beat strings:

Ex 14

It sounds like an allusion to Bloch, but after only four bars this lugubrious scrap of a tune is magically dismissed by woodwind and timpani, who insist on D major. After this there are no more shadows; the final section is an exuberant tarantella, and the concerto ends with a joyous shout from the brass.

Unlike the Violin Concerto, this fine work received only one performance in over 30 years, at a BBC Contemporary Music

Concert on 13 May 1952. Originally the Cello Concerto was to have been conducted by Ernest Ansermet, but John Pritchard was asked to step in at the last moment, so that there was little chance of consultation between composer and conductor. In addition, Goffredo Petrassi appropriated most of the rehearsal time for his own *Second Concerto for Orchestra*. Listening to a recording of this first performance was a frustrating experience; how welcome therefore were the 1985 and subsequent broadcasts of the work by Alexander Baillie with the BBC Philharmonic Orchestra under Edward Downes, and how satisfying that everyone can now hear these artists' fine interpretation on record.

Max Rostal and Bernard preparing the first performance of the
violin concerto in 1946.

4

The Violin Concerto
Max Rostal

It is nearly six years now since the death of my dear and admired friend BERNARD STEVENS – a very great loss to me personally and to the musical world in general. Eleven years younger than myself, he was only 66 when he died. I have lost many close friends over the years, and although I know this is to be expected at my time of life, I still cannot come to terms with these bereavements. Among them are the British composers Arnold Bax, Arthur Benjamin, Benjamin Britten, Francis Chagrin, Benjamin Frankel, Constant Lambert, E. J. Moeran, Franz Reizenstein, Matyas Seiber, William Walton, Ralph Vaughan Williams – and now Bernard Stevens. These friends were a valued and integral part of my life. Perhaps this is the penalty of being a survivor!

I first met Bernard when he came with his charming and gifted young fiancée, Bertha, for her audition to study with me during the Second World War. They played the Violin Sonata which he had written for her, and I was immediately struck by the quality of the music of this young composer. We continued to meet at the interesting meetings in London of the newly formed Committee (now Society) for the Promotion of New Music. We were interested in each other right from the beginning, and our acquaintanceship grew into a very warm and enduring friendship. After I left England for Switzerland for health reasons in 1958, our meetings were understandably not as frequent as they had been during the years of my residence in London; however, we still continued to meet at the Royal College of Music, where Bernard was a professor of composition, whenever I visited England.

I was fortunate enough to observe at close range the various stages on his way to fame, and I therefore choose to write a little about my personal relationship and experience of working with Bernard.

After I had become acquainted with some of his works, I tentatively asked Bernard whether the idea of writing a violin concerto for me might appeal to him. He was attracted by the idea,

BERNARD STEVENS

CONCERTO

for

VIOLIN & ORCHESTRA

Arranged for Violin & Piano

The Violin part edited by Max Rostal

To Max,
in admiration and gratitude
for your wonderful perform
Bernard Steve
12.5.48.

ALFRED LENGNICK & CO. LTD.

14 Berners Street, London. W.

Sole Selling Agents for Canada of
The Frederick Harris Music Co. Limited
Oakville, Ontario, Canada

and he worked on the concerto while stationed in Bournemouth in the Army. This fine work was completed on 2 February 1943, when the composer was only 27 – in my opinion a remarkable achievement for such a young man, in view of the astonishing maturity, profundity, superior technique and imagination of the work. True, we saw a great deal of each other during the creation of this lovely concerto, and I am proud to say that he frequently accepted some of my ideas. Although Bernard knew exactly what he wanted, his modest and charming character always enabled him to be open to suggestions; this close collaboration gave me great pleasure, and I was very happy to perform this concerto whenever the opportunity presented itself. We received letters of high praise for the work from eminent musicians following these performances.

One of the many interesting aspects of this violin concerto is the opening theme, which consists of a twelve-tone row which Bernard actually invented much earlier when he was still a student at Cambridge. He used the theme in a Toccata and Fugue written in 1936, later adapting it for the Violin Concerto. I quote the two versions:

TOCCATA AND FUGUE

The Sonata for Violin and Piano, though an earlier work, was
not published until 1948, at the same time as the Violin Concerto,
though by a different publisher. I was asked to edit the Sonata, as
I had been in the case of the Concerto, and I well remember the
pleasure I had in doing it. I first performed this charming work
in public with the composer at a Concert of the Committee for
the Promotion of New Music in London in 1943. Further concert
performances followed and also broadcasts from the BBC and other
radio stations.

I find it hard to understand why so many violinists – and
particularly the younger generation of British violinists – appear to
ignore such fine violin works as these. Is there really no place for
anything except 'avant-garde' music – which most audiences do not
enjoy anyway? I strongly believe in Bernard Stevens' works, and
I greatly wish that they were known to a much wider circle than
has been the case up till now. I myself have performed his works
in England and in various countries of Europe with considerable
success.

I should like to close with a quotation from Colin Mason's article
on Bernard Stevens in *Grove's Dictionary of Music* which expresses
an opinion with which I emphatically agree: 'The seriousness,
integrity and personal distinction of his music make him one of
the most important British composers of his generation'.

5
Reflections on the Cello Concerto
William Pleeth

It was early in 1984 that I was made aware that a tape-recording of the Cello Concerto by Bernard Stevens had been made and was available.

This was taken from my broadcast in 1952 of a BBC Contemporary Music concert with the Royal Philharmonic Orchestra under John Pritchard, who took the place of Ernest Ansermet at short notice.

Hearing the work again after so many years gave me the renewed opportunity to think back on Stevens the man and the musician – a bird's eye view back through time, if you like!

My first thoughts regarding this highly gifted composer were of his humanity and his lack of self-importance – the latter quality making him 'everybody's man' among musicians and non-musicians alike.

Listening to the concerto again made me greatly aware and somewhat sad that no further performances had followed mine, for my impression of this hearing over thirty years later made a great impact on me. It is a work of great inner passion – a full-scale work in every sense of the word – which calls for great involvement.

Looking back on this first performance, which was created in only one single short rehearsal, my great regret is that opportunities for further performance* – which would have enabled the work to be recognised for its true stature – were so long delayed.

I can only hope that several of today's excellent young cellists will include this work in their repertoire, for it is surely among the finest concertos written during the last fifty years or more.

---

* The *Cello Concerto* has now been recorded by Alexander Baillie (see Discography).

6

The Chamber Music
Malcolm MacDonald

Music for chamber ensembles occupies a full quarter of Bernard Stevens' output, and the works are consistently distributed through his catalogue of compositions from his op.1 to the *Autumn Sequence*, op.52, written just over two years before his death. In the last months of his life he was planning, among other things, a new violin sonata, and *A Meditation on a Theme of Shostakovich*, for solo viola and string quartet. It is plain that he was strongly drawn to the chamber medium, for its possibilities of vigorous dialectical argument and intimate expression; and in it he produced several of his most characteristic and important scores.

The first work which Stevens felt worthy to bear an opus number was his Sonata for Violin and Piano, written and first performed at the R.C.M. by Stevens and Hans Geiger, winning him the 1940 Parry Prize. It is, indeed, the first notable milestone of his composing career. The Sonata was written for and dedicated to his future wife, Bertha; and her playing of it so impressed Max Rostal that he invited the young composer to write a Violin Concerto for him.

One can see why Rostal was so impressed. There is no trace of the 'prentice piece' about the Sonata; in its sombre lyricism, passion, rhythmic drive, and formal cogency it already presents a youthful statement of what were to remain its composer's characteristic virtues. It is in a single concise movement, ternary in structure though owing a fair amount to sonata form: the outer sections are dominated by the long-breathed *cantabile* melody from which most of the work's material is derived, while the piano plays a discreetly accompanimental rôle (save that its bass is always thematically important). The central, developmental section is faster and more active, with the two instruments competing on more equal terms; the texture is less contrapuntal than we shall find in later Stevens works, but there are plenty of pointers to the future, such as the splendid canon at figure 7. The moment of recapitulation is beautifully handled: the

Sonata's opening material returns practically verbatim, but wholly transfigured through change of register (violin two octaves up) and texture (violin muted, for the only time in the work). The coda is pensive, finally turning the Sonata's uneasy tonality (a minor-ish A with a prominent tritone) towards a quiet, reflective A major. The whole work speaks with an authority and stylistic integration that belie its composer's years, and its considerable promise was amply fulfilled in the superb Piano Trio, op.3 of two years later.

Like the Sonata, the Trio was composed somewhat under the influence of Stevens' early enthusiasm for the music of Ernest Bloch – but this is apparent at a technical level, not in any lack of individual personality. Written in 1942 (amazingly, part of it while the composer was in bed with influenza!), the Trio was awarded the Clements Memorial Fund Prize in that year, was premièred at the Wigmore Hall in 1943, and was revised for publication in 1948, when it was played at the Cheltenham Festival. It's in three movements, the second and third of which are played without a break, and the whole work projects an essentially continuous argument. This echoes the Violin Sonata on a larger formal scale, and there are also affinities with it in the tonal situation at the outset: the piano's restless, motoric quaver *ostinato* outlines a sort of D minor with an important tritone. But immediately this has structural consequences – the first movement's main theme (Ex.1a) is stated by fugal entries, answered at the tritone, G sharp, over the continuing bass *ostinato*.

Ex.1

(a) Allegro deciso

(b) (Violin)

(c) Adagio ♩=42

(d) Allegro con brio ♩=152

The piano trio is a more difficult medium than may be commonly supposed; the three instruments do not blend very well, and our century has seen few really successful examples: the Ravel, the Rebecca Clarke, the second Shostakovich, the second Frank Bridge, Alan Bush's *Concert Studies* and, undoubtedly, Bernard Stevens' op.3. Its first movement gives the impression of having been composed in a single rush of inspiration. Ex.1a gives rise to a sonata-like structure of controlled, exciting energy, characterised by thrusting, sinewy counterpoint. The pace seldom slackens, and when it does – just for a little – for more contrastingly expressive material, those themes (such as the nominal 'second subject', Ex.1b) inevitably prove on examination to be variations of the opening idea. The movement is to all intents and purposes monothematic, the ruthlessly logical working-out of a single conception – with the heady, thrilling quality that such logical processes sometimes have.

Lyrical expansion is given its proper place in the slow movement, a calm song for the string instruments over quietly-pulsing piano chords. But the thematic ideas directly continue the argument of the first movement: the main tune (Ex.1c) is another clear variant of 1a, as is the line that answers it in the deep bass of the piano. The tritone relationship is now exploited in a different way: the violin's second statement of 1c is on F sharp, against a cello answer on C. The finale, which follows without a break, is based on a *giocoso* variant of the work's opening theme (Ex.1d) and returns to the restlessly contrapuntal texture of that movement, but with occasional suggestions of march and fanfare. A more *contabile* second theme is given in duple time across the basic 3/4, before a modified recapitulation, and a brief coda which finally confirms the overall tonality as D major, and brings the movement to an end with a swiftness and punctuality that avoids all rhetoric. This Piano Trio is a work that has already stood the test of time: its economy, technical command, and downright directness of expression make a strong impression more than 40 years after it was composed.

The crowning achievement among this early group of chamber works, however, is the *Theme and Variations* for string quartet, op.11, completed in March 1949 and first presented at the Cheltenham Festival in that year. This is a score very rich in ideas, a large and complex structure whose every nook and cranny is packed with musical substance. Though not titled as such, it is

in effect Stevens' First String Quartet – a fact which was tacitly
confirmed when the composer, in 1962, explicitly named the
quartet he wrote in that year his Second.

The work is cast in a single large movement which consists of a
Theme, eleven Variations, and a Finale (numbered Variation XII)
whose texture is largely fugal. However, the composer regarded
this structure as actually containing four continuous 'movements',
each formed by a group of the variations. Hans Keller, reviewing
the piece for *Music Review*, hazarded the existence of a third formal
level, that of a rondo scheme cutting across the variation-groups,
articulated by those variations which contained the most explicit
reappearances of the theme.

The slow theme (Ex.2) is a noble inspiration: the tonal trajectory of its two constituent phrases – from E flat to its opposite, A, and back again – seems to be a further development of the tritone polarities seen in the other works so far discussed, and gives scope and justification for the wide-ranging tonal argument of the work as a whole. The theme's subsequent treatment shows Stevens to be in full command of all the potentialities of the quartet medium.

The 'first movement' (in the composer's scheme) consists of the theme itself and Variations I–V. Variation V is at the *Adagio* pace of the theme, balancing it, but the other four are much quicker – I and II *Allegretto*, lyrical and flowing, sharing the phrases of the theme among the instruments, with hints of neo-Elizabethan polyphony; and III and IV *Allegro*, more acid and angular, splitting the theme up into smaller rhythmic and melodic fragments with wide contrasts of register and dynamic. IV is a brilliant and witty *pizzicato* study. Variation V, when it arrives, proves to be music of great intensity, with an augmented *cantabile* version of the theme against a sarabande-like rhythmic pattern; the tonality is now B major, the theme moving at its mid-point to the tritonal opposite pole, F.

The 'second movement' (Variations VI–VIII) does duty for a capricious scherzo. The *Allegretto* Var VI uses fragments of the theme as accompaniment to a new melody – which is in fact a retrograde (in pitch, not rhythm) of Ex. 2, phrase by phrase. Var VII (*Poco più mosso*) reverses this process in all senses except that of pitch: the accompanimental patterns now use fragments of the theme in retrograde, while the theme itself, the right way round, is played against them in long note values. The emotional temperature rises and explodes into the *Presto* Variation VIII, where the violins and viola give out a very fast, *saltato* version of the theme against *pizzicato* cello interruptions in triplet cross-rhythm.

Variations IX-XI together form a 'slow movement', beginning *Adagio* with Variation IX which features *pesante* imitative writing in hard-bitten double-dotted rhythms between first and second violins, with something of the character of a Beethovenian funeral march. This leads, in Variation X, to a remote, withdrawn-sounding exact inversion of both the theme and its harmonization: as Hans Keller has pointed out (*loc.cit.*) this variation, in its closeness to the original theme, balances Variation V, and it also shares that variation's F-B tonal axis, suggesting a 'rondo' scheme at work in the over-all structure. Something of Variation V's character is preserved into the sublime Variation XI, a slow canon by inversion at the twelfth between first violin and viola (i.e. these instruments begin an octave plus a tritone apart), to which second violin and cello provide simultaneous high and low pedals. Towards the end the music gathers momentum, impelling us into the extended Variation XII which functions as the finale to the whole work.

This is an *Allegro deciso* fugue on a completely new subject, sprightly and highly rhythmical, announced at once by the viola. It is a daring stroke to introduce such fresh material so late in what has been a very strict argument, but the effect is satisfying, broadening the scope of the work as a whole. The fugue is thoroughly and excitingly worked out, with several contrasting episodes, until the crown of the composition is reached in a sonorous combination of the fugue subject with the original theme. Symmetry and logic thus satisfied, a grand conclusion is attained in E flat major.

If we may speak of a 'First Period' in Stevens' output, this *Theme and Variations* certainly brought it to a triumphant end. For the next three years he wrote no chamber music, unless we except his brief and rousing Two Fanfares for Four Natural Trumpets op.12, played by the Trumpeters of the Household Cavalry at the 1949 Cambridge Arts Festival – music for no imaginable 'chamber' but for the open and echoing air.

Stevens once remarked: 'When I was young, I had the mistaken notion that a work needed to be in one movement if it was to achieve continuity of thought and unity of structure', and the three main works we have so far considered were indeed single-movement designs; even the Piano Trio is so in essence, a kind of expansion of the Violin Sonata's ternary form. All three, moreover, were adaptations of sonata procedures to provide a satisfying unification of disparate expressive impulses. The works of the next few years continued to show a concern with one-movement forms, but sought their unity in other means of organization. It is notable that between 1949 and 1953 Stevens composed four works entitled 'Fantasia', two of which fall within the scope of this chapter. There can be little doubt that his ultimate inspiration in these pieces was the extended instrumental fantasia as cultivated by the Elizabethan composers. In their hands (and especially in Byrd's) the Fantasia had affinities with variation-form, but was much freer, more purely concerned with the reconciliation of broad contrasts into a scheme of unbroken continuity. It is obvious why this should have appealed to Stevens. Indeed three of his four Fantasias,[1] starting with the piano duet *Fantasia on the Irish 'Ho-Hoane'* (1949), actually take themes of the Elizabethan period as their starting-point.

The exception is the remarkable *Fantasia for Two Violins and Piano* op.20, written in 1952 for Sybil Copeland and Jack Glickman, and premièred by them with Arvon Davies at the piano in London in that year (on the same day as his daughter Catherine was born). Even here there seems to be, in wholly 20th century terms, an echo of Elizabethan practice. The basis of the *Fantasia* is not so much a theme as the opening slow chain of rising fourths (Ex.3*a*). No composer can now write such a chain without reminding an audience of Schoenberg's First Chamber Symphony, but Stevens' later treatment of this idea suggests that he had in mind those Elizabethan Fantasias which concern themselves with scalic formulae, such as Byrd's *Ut Re Mi* and various 'hexachord' pieces. This is partly confirmed by the piano's brooding descending-scale figures throughout much of the rest of the sombre *Adagio* first section.

Fourths are accordingly prominent in the chief subject of the ensuing *Allegro deciso* (Ex.3*b*) which has already appeared in doubled note-values in the *Adagio*; the other main element in the tune (marked x in the example) derives from a subsidiary idea in the first section. This is wiry, agile, combative music, at first presented in vigorous dialogue by the two violins. A *poco meno mosso* moves us

[1] I except from these remarks the much later *Fantasia for organ*, op.39, of 1966, which I do not know.

into $^6/_8$ time, with the second violin carrying a new *cantabile* tune developed from figure *x*, against dancing figuration in the other instruments. A gentle jig-like melody, *cantabile ma tranquillo*, is contrasted with the spikier writing in this section and eventually brings a brief, *pianissimo* recall of the opening *Adagio*. The *Allegro deciso* material returns and is worked up to a thrilling climax that bubbles over into fast triplet motion. A massive restatement of Ex.3a, the violins now playing in *ff sostenuto* octaves, brings the work to a majestic close in a finally unclouded C major.

The following year Stevens wrote another piece that he entitled Fantasia – his fine *Fantasia on Giles Farnaby's Dream*, perhaps the best-known of his solo piano works – and then went on to produce yet another, for violin and piano. The *Fantasia on a Theme of Dowland*, op.23 (dedicated to and first performed by Suzanne Rozsa and Paul Hamburger) makes an excellent complement to the Farnaby Fantasia, and is in fact one of Stevens' most delightful instrumental works. The theme he chose is characteristic not so much of John Dowland's famous melancholy but rather of his less celebrated high spirits: his Galliard *Can Shee Excuse*. This is generally performed as a quick, merry piece, but Stevens first introduces the tune – after a brooding cadenza-like introduction for violin alone – as a broad, noble *Adagio*; and throughout the opening portion of the work the two instruments continue to explore and extend it in this same grave, meditative spirit, and explore, too, the tune's characteristic flexible alternation between the metres of ³/₄ and ⁶/₈. There follows a lively, scherzando-like *Allegro* which presents variations of the tune, first wholly in ⁶/₈, then wholly in ³/₄, and then returns to ⁶/₈ for a further *leggiero* variation. The rhythmic excitement continues to increase in the next two variations, respectively in ²/₄ and ⁶/₁₆, with much *spiccato* and *staccato* writing for the two instruments. The work's emotional climax is in a trio of intense *Adagio* variations, the first two of which re-shape the tune into a ⁵/₈ metre, the last a noble three-part invention in ³/₄. A bright concluding *Allegro* finally displays the tune in its traditional galliard character, to end the work with vivacity and elegant wit. None of Stevens' works could really be termed 'difficult' to appreciate, but this *Fantasia* is among the most accessible of all, and one might have expected it to have taken its place in the general repertoire long ere now.

He followed it in 1954 with a short composition for brass quintet, the *Two Improvisations on Folksongs*, op.24. As always when he worked with borrowed themes, Stevens treated them with respect, affection, and a sometimes sceptical humour. 'Lowlands, my Lowlands' conceals various shafts of canonic erudition, and culminates in a sonorous chorale; 'The Cutty Wren' is made the subject of a witty fugal invention, the tune being pitted against itself with entries in progressively longer and longer note-values.

After this there was another break from chamber music, until in 1958 there appeared the *Lyric Suite* for string trio, op.30. This is the first sizeable chamber work in which Stevens managed to depart from his 'single-movement' obsession, since it has five movements whose 'real unity' (as he was later to write of his Second String Quartet) 'is not dependent on . . . external features but springs from conviction and purpose'. Nonetheless, the principles of thematic transformation and variation from one movement to another continue to play an important role in securing that unity. As its title suggests, the *Lyric Suite* steers well clear of sonata procedures and proportions, and its models seem more likely to have been Baroque than Berg, though its language is firmly 20th century and displays, indeed, a measure of interest in twelve-note possibilities.

A short 'Introduzione', marked *Adagio liberamente*, is dark-hued and thoughtful in tone, presenting all three instruments muted, the violin and viola feeling their way towards a thematic statement by means of small fragments of scale in close harmony and contrary motion. The result of their efforts metamorphoses into the main theme of the ensuing Scherzo – a hectic, bubbling virtuoso movement in $9/8$ – and scalic figures (often with octave displacement) are a central source of material for the rest of the work. There follows an 'Intermezzo' based on a long, sinuously extended *cantabile* melody whose rhythmic simplicity belies its harmonic sophistication: its first calm, long-breathed phrase states nine different pitches of the chromatic scale before repeating any of them. The fourth movement, a short polyphonic invention headed 'Passacaglietta', shows a similar development: its ground bass is related to the Intermezzo theme and consists of 13 notes, though only nine different pitches, because of repetitions of its opening note D, which Stevens causes to function as a clear tonal centre. The Passacaglietta forms an introduction to a final bright, capricious fugue, at whose climax – in a coup reminiscent of the *Theme and Variations* – the ground of the Passacaglietta is imposed upon the fugue subject to precipitate a resolute close in D minor.

That Stevens – one of the most open-minded (which is to say large-minded) composers of his time – should have shown interest in aspects of serialism should come as no surprise: one of the principal characteristics of his music, throughout his career, seems to have been the search for ever new but always musically valid principles of formal integration. The *Theme and Variations* is full of subtle feats of inversion and retrogradation: techniques which are in truth as old as polyphonic music itself, though they acquired new impetus in the early 20th century at the hands of the Second Viennese School. They can be found in frequent, unobtrusive use elsewhere in Stevens' output, not least in the *Lyric Suite* – and the *Suite* had in addition displayed a tendency towards a highly chromatic linear style. The logical next step was some undogmatic measure of serialism, with all twelve notes in play, and this is what we find as the basis of Stevens' next chamber work, the String Quartet No.2, op.34, of 1962 – the work which, if I was forced into such an invidious choice, I would probably rank as his chamber music masterpiece.

In a programme-note for the Quartet – from which I have already quoted his remarks on the 'mistaken notion' about one-movement forms he had when younger – Stevens set out its structural foundation as follows:

> The harmonic basis of the whole work consists of four triads, two major and two minor, that together make up a twelve-note row without repetitions. Each movement uses the four triads in a different order and transposed to a different tonality. This sort of note-row, far from being a way to ensure strict atonality, as required by Schoenberg and Webern, does, I hope, give the work a firm tonal basis. I realise that Schoenberg and Webern (but probably not Berg) would have disapproved of this heretical interpretation of the creed, but I am comforted by the thought that Schoenberg said somewhere that in twelve-note composition, the composition was more important than the twelve-notes.

Personally speaking, I doubt that Schoenberg, who abominated the term 'atonality', would have been troubled in the least by Stevens' personal application of elements of twelve-note technique: he would be more likely to have paid attention to its true compositional virtues, its powerful ideas, their superb working-out, and the easy mastery of the quartet medium. As he himself said (in that 'somewhere' that Stevens had hazily remembered):[2]

> I can't say it often enough: my works are twelve-note *compositions*, not *twelve-note* compositions . . . I still don't care to be regarded as a constructor on account of the bit of juggling I can do with series, because that would be doing too little to deserve it. I think more has to be done to deserve such a title . . .

Stevens' procedures in his Second Quartet simply illustrate the extraordinary fertility of Schoenberg's basic idea, which is capable of exploration in many different directions.

His methods are, as we shall see, considerably more complex and flexible than he gives himself credit for in his brief explication; and the Quartet, as well as being a singularly beautiful piece of music, is surely one of the most elegant successes, among the many attempts by composers, to write 'serial' music which retains a strong basis in diatonic tonality.

From the first movement's calm *Andante* introduction there

---

[2] Letter to Rudolf Kolisch, 27 July 1932.

emerges a long lyrical *cantabile* theme on first violin, with accompaniment from viola and cello, that announces Stevens' version of serialism in its most straightforward terms:

Ex.4

Here the basis of the four triads is very simply seen, as is the freedom of Stevens' approach. It should be noted that (to fill the total chromatic space) the pair of major triads are an augmented fourth apart, as are the pair of minor ones – which gives Stevens ample scope for exploring the tritonal relationships that so attracted him in earlier works. It can also be seen (comparing melody and accompaniment) that he treats each triad as a germinal cell in its own right, not merely as a segment of an unalterable series: the order of notes within each triad is not fixed (nor is the order of the triads themselves), so long as that triad is fully articulated before passing to the next. This means that Stevens is enabled to exploit semitonal and leading-note movement from one triad to another, and through this he develops a contrasting chain of thought, in conjunct motion by tones and semitones, which throughout forms a highly chromatic linear foil to his main subject-matter. He is further able to make each triad function as a root in the strictly key-centred sense, and indeed to give one of the four a 'quasi-tonic' primacy over the other three so that there is a firm tonal basis to the Quartet's over-all structure. (It has the feel of a work 'in C', with first and last movements orientated to that key; the scherzo and slow movement are 'in' B minor and E minor respectively.) The processes can be analysed in detail throughout the Quartet, but the scope and nature of the present essay precludes any exhaustive approach; however, examples from the four movements will give some idea of the variety of music which Stevens wrings from these premises.

The entire first movement is concerned with the development of Ex.4. The treatment is especially searching with regard to rhythm, for the basic 'row' is pressed into ever livelier and livelier shapes as the tempo is progressively increased. There is much passion in the music, which rises to an exalted climax with the Ex.4 melody in its original form (though at a different transposition) on first violin in octaves, while the other instruments supply the harmony of the basic triads, also in octaves, *fortissimo*, in pulsing rhythm. After this the movement subsides to a peaceful close.

The second movement is a *Presto* scherzo, emerging at first in whispers on muted violin and viola (Ex.5a). It rapidly develops into a dazzling *furioso* display-piece, frequently characterized by torrential semiquaver patterns and virtuoso deployment of the ensemble, with much rugged syncopation and closely-argued canonic writing. It also makes thoroughgoing use of the 'chromatic counterfoil' I mentioned earlier: while 5a is its first theme, a second subject appears as Ex.5b – the cello melody being forged out of the tone-semitone links between the triads, while the triads themselves act as an explosive chordal accompaniment.

The texture is largely polyphonic throughout, until a whirlwind coda that ends in a forceful variant of 5b, with all the instruments in octaves.

Thereafter the serene third movement, *Adagio*, opens with peaceful descending phrases spelling out the triads over the entire

Ex.5

tessitura of the four instruments. This forms the introduction to the emotional heart of the Quartet, a slow chaconne which begins:

Ex.6

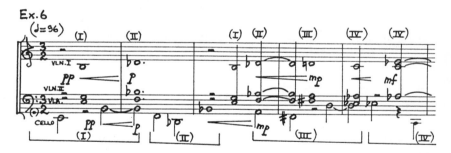

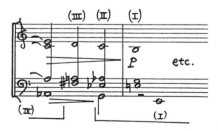

This dark-hued, noble music is among Stevens' finest inspirations. The chords above the cello theme (which, it will be noted, present the basic triads in original and then retrograde form) become the basis of an intense, chromatic development. The chaconne, however, gradually becomes less strict: first an austere chordal theme, not unrelated to the scherzo theme Ex.5*b*, is introduced on second violin and viola; and after this a marked pause brings a *poco più mosso*. Here the music is centred more on the opposite tonal pole of B flat minor, with the chaconne theme appearing in shorter variants, before the Ex.6 chords are used as accompaniment to a long, rhapsodic first violin melody. Then the violin itself takes up the chaconne theme in its highest register: the music gathers speed, the tension rises, and the *Allegro* finale begins without a break.

This is closely related to the first movement, but is even more vigorous: Ex. 7 is its main theme.

Ex.7   Allegro (♩=72)

There is something of the scherzo in the movement's character, and several reminiscences of Ex.5*b* occur among the hectic semi-quaver figurations. Eventually the tempo increases to *Presto*, and the cello states the original Ex.4, *cantabile*, in syncopation against the other three instruments. A decisive coda presents the first movement theme in canon and diminution on all the instruments, converging on a trenchant statement of its first germinal cell and a resounding octave C.

Although the 'triadic serialism' Stevens employed in the Second Quartet had been outstandingly successful, he seems to have regarded the method as a unique technical solution to the challenges of a particular work, not to be repeated. He continued to explore new organizational principles, including the incorporation of some serial ideas into tonal contexts when the individual work seemed to call for it. However, with the *Trio for Violin, Horn, and Piano*, op.38, of 1966 we are back on familiar ground as far as harmonic and motivic development are concerned.

The work was conceived partly as a companion-piece to Brahms' Trio for the same combination, and indeed the germinal impulse behind its thematic material is to be found in the Brahms, specifically in the rising and falling fifths and thirds of the second theme of Brahms' second movement. But there is no literal quotation: the only composer of whom we are likely to be reminded is Stevens himself. In both its polyphonic style, and its formal scheme of three movements played without a break, the work does display certain affinities with his early op.3 Piano Trio.

A brief rhapsodic piano solo – marked 'quasi Cadenza' and displaying the work's salient intervallic cells as well as a prominent semitonal mordent that is to become omnipresent – acts as introduction to the spacious first movement. This is a ternary design centred on B flat, whose first calm span is a beautifully-poised *Adagio*, all three instruments taking part in an expressive contrapuntal discussion on equal terms. Contrast is deliberately excluded, and this in itself gives rise to tensions which are released in the movement's central *Allegro*, a splendid piece of fast music, *echt*-Stevens in its pulsating rhythmic drive. Now the instruments are strongly differentiated: violin and horn share thematic material, but the horn's versions of the material tend to be expanded into broader note-values; the piano's rôle here, though still thematic, is more accompanimental, keeping up the rhythmic excitement. The music builds to a fast and furious climax, from which a cascade of quavers from the piano brings about a compressed recapitulation of the *Adagio*, much tenser than before, the material being rhythmically varied. All three instruments climb higher and higher in their registers, until a high F on the violin carries directly over into the second movement.

This is still *Adagio* as it begins, and is comparatively brief, though the tempo fluctuates as the movement takes the form of a joint cadenza for violin and horn in dialogue, without any contribution from the piano. As a cadenza, it continues to discuss material familiar to us from the first movement (both its slower and faster sections), and towards the end effectively pits the two instruments against each other in contrary motion, contrasting the lowest register of the horn with the highest of the violin. Without a break they pass straight into the finale, where the piano re-enters with a bubbling dance-like tune in ⁵/₈. Stevens himself described the tune as 'featuring the unsymmetrical rhythms characteristic of Slav folk music', but did not specify more exactly what country's folk-music he may have had in mind. In any case this theme becomes the subject of a cheerfully athletic rondo (with rhythmic episodes in constantly-changing time signatures) which serves the work excellently as a finale. Chains of thirds (which the previous movements, in their concern with fanfare-like fifths, had not dwelt upon the such an extent) become important here, though there are disguised references to the first movement as well. The work ends in high spirits and high good humour, with motivic unanimity and an uncontested E flat tonality.

The following year saw the composition of a work for the largest chamber ensemble Stevens ever employed: the *Suite for 6 Instruments*, op.40. The ensemble, however, was not of his choosing – the *Suite* was commissioned by the Tilford Bach Society for a première in the context of a concert including two Bach cantatas, and the six instruments specified were flute, oboe, violin, viola da gamba, cello, and harpsichord.[3] Stevens in fact uses the whole ensemble only in the first and last of the four movements; the second is confined to string instruments and keyboard, and the third is a trio for flute, oboe and keyboard. Although, as befitted the occasion, the *Suite* is generously provided with Baroque gestures, on a deeper structural level it shows his continued probing of the possibilities of serialism within the context of diatonic tonality. The key-centres of the various movements form a circle of major thirds, A – F – C sharp – A, but each movement makes some use of a twelve-note 'motto-theme' (Ex.8). Whereas the String Quartet No.2 had employed a note-row made up of four triads, this theme – and it is clearly as a *theme* that Stevens uses it throughout, not as a complete grow-bag for melody and harmony – consists of four separate 'stacks' of perfect fourths. It is announced at the outset of the first movement – which, like the Horn Trio, begins with a prominent Baroque-style mordent.

The first movement has something of the character of a

---

[3] For subsequent performances Stevens specified viola and piano as acceptable alternatives to viola da gamba and harpsichord.

Ex.8

French overture, with its outer sections impassioned yet formal, making much use of the massed ensemble and antiphony between wind and strings. There is no change of tempo, but the central portion is more lyrical and free-flowing, characterised by smaller note-values and smaller ensembles, and so has a different sense of motion. The 'motto theme' Ex.8 is the subject of discussion throughout, and towards the end is presented as more of a 'row', in even crotchets.

The second movement, *Allegro deciso*, is a lively double fugue in 4/4 whose first theme (entrusted mainly to the strings and marked 'modo classico') is very distantly derived from Ex.8, and the second theme, announced by the harpsichord, is much closer to it – but incorporates the semitonal mordent of the very opening as well. The contrapuntal activity bubbles over into a harpsichord cadenza combining fragments of both themes before a coda in which the themes are shared between harpsichord and strings. There follows an *Andante* slow movement which, while mainly in $^5/4$ (the various movements are metrically progressive – the finale will be in $^6/8$), has the feel of a grave, elegiac Sarabande. The thematic interest here is divided between ascending and descending chains of thirds adumbrated in the harpsichord's solo introduction, and a very clear variant of the Ex.8 motto-theme in the flute and oboe – it is merely altered rhythmically to fit the movement's character. The writing here is beautifully poised, with a sharp clarity of instrumentation that completely cancels any notion of pastiche Baroque-ery.

The finale has a weighty *Adagio* introduction, with stern melody on the strings, decorated by keyboard flourishes: but this soon spills over into the finale proper, an *Allegro* Gigue whose main theme re-mixes the fourths of Ex.8 to produce a breezy tune that proves equal to all the contrapuntal paces Stevens contrives to put it through. As in his other works, emotional relaxation does not imply intellectual relaxation, or diminishment of contrapuntal skill.

It's possible (though it's also easy to make too much of the distinction) to see Stevens' output of chamber music as falling into four chronological groups, the first and third of which are concerned with more standard forms, while the second and fourth show a relaxation into freer structures (and tend to concentrate on smaller ensembles). Thus in the 1940s we have a Sonata, a Trio, and a Quartet in the form of Theme and Variations, which were followed in the early 1950s by two violin Fantasias and the short Improvisations. Then between 1958 and 1967 there is a reversion to classical forms with two Suites, another Trio, and another Quartet. The final group of works, written in the decade 1970-80, turns away once more from classical archetypes: there are two instrumental solos, one of them a 'Ballad' and the other an Improvisation, and finally a duo which is explicitly, and most unclassically, entitled a 'Sequence'. Physically they are fairly small works; in this final period Stevens' energies were more often turned to major orchestral scores and his opera on *The Shadow of the Glen*. But they are no less absorbing and affecting for all that.

The *Ballad* for guitar, op.45, subtitled *The Bramble Briar*, was written for the Italian guitarist Angelo Gilardino in 1971, though premièred by Carlos Bonell in Britain. It has some affinities with the two Ballads which Stevens had already composed for piano, and also with the group of instrumental Fantasias on borrowed themes that date from the early 1950s. But its opening also shows that the sounds of the *Suite* and the *Horn Trio* were still in the composer's mind:

Ex.9

Here the guitar's natural tuning almost inevitably led Stevens to think in terms of ascending and descending fourths; and once again we encounter the semitone mordent of the *Suite* and *Trio*, used here as a pivot from one chain of fourths to another. These are austere and rather sinister sounds, and they dominate the rhapsodic introductory portion of the work – rightly, for 'The Bramble Briar' itself, whose tune is presently stated in a relatively innocent A major, is a Somerset folksong telling of murder, ghosts, and a body in a ditch. Stevens' work develops into a series of free variations on the tune, with much use of elements of Ex.9 as contrast. Written with obvious understanding of and love for the sonorities of the guitar, it develops into a piece requiring considerable virtuosity. But there is always a dark side to its flashing bravura, and it ends in a tragic variant of Ex.9, the semitone mordent now sounding bitter at the bottom of the texture.

Effective solo guitar works, however, are not all that thin on the ground; substantial pieces for unaccompanied viola are prodigiously rare, and that tiny repertoire was greatly enriched by the appearance of Stevens' op.48, the *Improvisation* for solo viola, composed in 1973 for his daughter Catherine, who eventually premièred it in a BBC broadcast in 1978.[4] Beautifully written for the instrument, and taxing the technical skills (and musicality) of the player to their limits, this impassioned ten-minute monologue makes no attempt to disguise or lighten the husky, soulful, serious voice of the viola. Rather it glories in the viola's characteristic sound, to project an intense and thoughtful discourse with maximum force.

The work is based on an opening theme which spans the entire range of the instrument and whose intervals open out gradually from a semitone to a major seventh and then close

up again. This theme is heard twice more, with developments at each appearance, and parts of it appear elsewhere in inversion. Dividing these statements are the 'improvisations' deriving from it and from its implied harmonies. These are free and frequently fantastic: a spectral 'À la valse' is especially noteworthy in this respect. Despite the frequent changes of register, tempo, and character the *tone* remains the same – not hectoring or exhortatory, but profoundly serious, infused with the passion of deeply-held convictions. Eventually there comes a freely fugal section in two voices which, despite its elements of fantasy, keeps returning to its principal subject in key after key. A quick coda sums up various elements explored throughout the work, and convinces us that, despite its 'improvisatory' manner, we have really been listening to an argument of the tautest intellectual fibre.

[4] After Stevens' death, a violin version, dedicated to Erich Gruenberg, was found among his papers, and stands as a valid alternative form of this work.

Seven years passed before Stevens composed what was to prove his last piece of chamber music, the *Autumn Sequence* for guitar and harpsichord, for Raymond Burley and Stephen Bell. A certain air of mystery hangs about it: its unusual and evocative instrumental combination and its rather aloof and quiescent mood seem to set it apart from his other music. It breathes, as it were, the air from a different spiritual sphere: its methods of construction remain bafflingly opaque. According to the composer it is 'based on' the two hexagrams for Autumn in the *I Ching* or Book of Changes, the ancient Chinese oracle in which Stevens became deeply interested towards the end of his life. But how based and to what musical ends?

Bertha Stevens has kindly allowed me to examine two pages from one of the composer's last sketchbooks: they carry some roughly-pencilled notations which clearly employ a method of composition relating to I Ching hexagrams. After careful study I have come to the conclusion that these particular sketches have no direct relation to *Autumn Sequence* (the hexagrams employed are in any case not the same): but insofar as I understand the method adumbrated, I do see that Stevens was able to use the four possible kinds of line ('Young' or 'Old' Yin and Yang) to generate six-note rhythmic patterns involving four different note-values, and six-chord harmonic sequences involving four possible kinds of triad – major, minor, augmented, and diminished.[5] I am unable to determine whether tonal roots and melodic lines were also generated by those methods, or whether there were further refinements (for instance, whether the numerological values traditionally assigned to the various lines played any part). Nor does it seem possible to analyse the harmonic and rhythmic structures of *Autumn Sequence* by applying to the two hexagrams for Autumn the pattern of equivalence that emerges from the sketchbook pages. But that *something of the sort* is operating in *Autumn Sequence* I have not the slightest doubt: the four triadic forms, for instance, practically saturate its harmony, and no one section uses more than four different note-values.

Better, in any case, to turn from these constructional specu-

[5] Immediately prior to *Autumn Sequence*, Stevens had composed his piano piece *Nocturne on a Note-Row by Ronald Stevenson*. This row (from Stevenson's Hugh MacDiarmid setting *The Skeleton of the Future*) is built up of the four possible triadic forms, and Stevens' work on the *Nocturne* may have carried over into his thinking when writing *Autumn Sequence*.

lations to the piece itself as music, and as an evocation – as it seems partly to be – of the poetic-oracular ideas associated with the Autumn hexagrams, which are *P'i* (Standstill, in the sense of stagnation) and *Kuan* (Contemplation). *P'i* is explained in the ancient Chinese texts as symbolizing decay, lack of understanding between men: an unfavourable time when the wise should withdraw into seclusion. *Kuan* indicates the moment between an invocation of the Deity and the making of a sacrifice: a sacred moment when what is required of one is the deepest inner concentration. These are images that chime with the 'melancholy' that has always been associated with Autumn: but as always with the *I Ching*, the images have a moral force that is the opposite of self-indulgence. Is this not also a characteristic of Stevens' music? In any case, as Bertha Stevens has said, it is fascinating how an 'eastern aura' results from his rather mysterious and ingenious adaptation of the Eastern prognostic art to Western musical practice.

Autumn Sequence is cast in a single movement; as its title implies, it has the feel of a freely-associating succession of moods and textures – though in fact it is as closely argued as any of Stevens' other works. There are two principal thematic elements: a wide-spanned idea, rising and falling in progressively decreasing note-values, announced at the outset by unaccompanied guitar: and a long, smoothly expressive melody shared between the two instruments immediately afterwards. It is the latter which is subjected to a series of fairly free variations; the former punctuates these with occasional reappearances in more recognisable form, each time more massively harmonised. The course of the work is capricious; short bursts of scurrying *scherzando* activity counterweighted by slower, inevitable-seeming progressions in even note-values. Stevens exploits the plangency of his two instruments to the utmost: the music is full of memorable sharp-sweet sounds, often in unusual polyrhythmic textures, and both harpsichord and guitar make play with that bitter neo-Baroque mordent which is a kind of Stevens fingerprint in the later chamber works. The tendency to build sections, rhythmically, out of a very few note-values – sometimes only one – is a new departure in Stevens' music, and becomes especially noticeable towards the close of the work. The coda – one of the most haunting pages Stevens ever penned – reconciles his new, presumably *I Ching*–derived, harmonic practice with all his old contrapuntal skill: a fine-spun, wonderfully flexible canon by inversion, around a tolling hypnotic succession of triads (minor, major, augmented, diminished) in a constant quaver rhythm:

Though *Autumn Sequence* was not the last work Stevens composed, one cannot help feeling an elegiac, valedictory quality about these bars, mingled with a curious kind of spiritual exaltation.

Stevens had available to him one of the most accessible *I Ching* texts, the Penguin edition translated by Alfred Douglas, and also the classic edition by Richard Wilhelm, which contains a fascinating introduction by C.G. Jung and is much fuller in its treatment of the hexagrams.[6] Wilhelm, in discussing the hexagram *Kuan*, notes that:

> A slight variation of tonal stress gives the Chinese name for this hexagram a double meaning. It means both contemplating and being seen, in the sense of being an example.

Autumn Sequence closes in profoundly contemplative mood. But in terms of this second meaning of *Kuan* it also constitutes an example, as does all of Bernard Stevens' chamber music, of the rarely-linked virtues of thorough craftsmanship, sensitivity of expression, and an inexhaustibly exploratory attitude to the stuff of music itself. Such examples endure, even through 'times of decay', to be an inspiration to future generations.

[6] Translation by C.F. Baynes, Routledge & Kegan Paul, 1951.

Left to right: William Alwyn, Sir John Barbirolli, Arnold Bax,
Edmund Rubbra, Bernard Stevens. Cheltenham 1951

With Antoinette and Edmund Rubbra at the Cheltenham Festival Club.

7

The Works for Small Orchestra
Harry Newstone

The directness of idiom that characterises so much of Bernard Stevens' music is a prime feature of his four works for string and chamber orchestras. The first three of them were written within a few years of one another in the mid-1940s, and the last more than a quarter-century later. Although there is no evidence to support such a conjecture, the three earlier works might have been conceived as a set, so comprehensively do they reflect the different aspects of the composer's attitudes, interests and individuality at that time – many of them to become hallmarks of his style.

The *Ricercar* for string orchestra was composed in 1944 and received its first performance in 1946 at a BBC concert in Warwick Castle, by the London String Orchestra conducted by Alan Bush. As the title implies, the work is an exercise in contrapuntal texture and it is surely not fortuitous that its first theme should show a barely hidden relationship to the theme by Frederick the Great upon which Bach based his *Musical Offering*, particularly as it appears in the magnificent six-part Ricercare of that work.

This theme (a) is closely worked out in formal fugal procedure, with stretto, inversion and chromatic harmony used to concentrate the argument and heighten the tension. At fig. 5 (Lengnick score) a new theme (b) marked *Più mosso* is introduced, characterised rhythmically by its group of four semi-quavers.

It, too, is developed with skill and imagination, at one point (fig. 9) splitting into 'doubled' lines, combining in mirror inversions. The *crescendo* to *fff* engendered by this process forms the work's central climax, and it dies down to introduce a third theme (c) which is related to (b) in tempo and to (a) in concealing within its shape the first five notes of the Bach theme, in its re-establishment of the home key of A minor.

A third fugue is developed, at the climax of which there seems but one logical thing to do, and in the short but powerful coda, themes (a), (b) and (c) are most effectively combined. It is abundantly clear from this excellent piece that, in his late twenties, Stevens was already not only a highly accomplished contrapuntist, but one who could indulge this skill without loss of expressive ability, a gift that was clearly recognised by those who reviewed the *Ricercar* when it first appeared. The critic of *Musical Opinion* wrote that 'The composer handles his forces with perfect assurance'; *Music and Letters* found the work 'deeply felt and musically moving and convincing'; and *Tempo* thought that it 'stands out as the best in a considerable batch of string works'.

The *Eclogue* for small orchestra, scored for flute, oboe, clarinet, bassoon, two horns, three timpani and strings was completed in 1946, and first performed the following year in the Royal Albert Hall at a London International Orchestra concert, conducted by Anatole Fistoulari who had commissioned it. A charming and atmospheric piece, it shows within a few bars that Stevens was as able to evoke the simplicities of a pastoral idyll as he was to present the complexities of fugal argument.

The implications of the title are immediately apparent with harmonically undulating strings providing a background for a series of woodwind dialogues. In its opening statement the solo oboe sets forth two of the ideas upon which the piece is built and from which others are derived.

Unlike (a), which doesn't change much when restated, (b)
re-appears in a number of different rhythmic guises, of which
Ex.5 gives two, without, however, losing its identity because of its
distinctive shape. After a short climax, a new idea is presented in

canon, first by horn and cellos, then by flute and bassoon.

The strings, which so far have assumed a subsidiary role,
come to the fore in an agitated central episode which develops the
material of (c) to a more extended climax, at the height of which
(a) and (b) are recapitulated, followed, as the mood returns to one
of tranquillity, by (c) in a dialogue between flute and oboe. A C
natural pedal undermines the E minor tonality, and is deflected to
F sharp for just long enough to establish that note as a dominant of
B, to which the pedal C sinks as a new tonic. The violins climb to a
B major chord that is quietly endorsed by the bassoon and horns.
The critics of *The Daily Mail* and *Musical Opinion* respectively
found the *Eclogue* 'of marked originality' and 'a fine, sincere, and
moving work'.

The *Sinfonietta* for string orchestra was written, to a BBC
commission, in 1948, two years after the *Eclogue*. With a number
of other commissions on hand at the time, the *Sinfonietta* was set
down in three weeks, and received its first performance the same
year in a broadcast by the Welbeck String Orchestra under Maurice
Miles. Stevens said that the enforced speed of writing for films was
a very good preparation for composing such a substantial work in
so short a time.

The *Sinfonietta* is in three movements: *Allegro volubilmente,
Adagio affettuoso* and *Allegro deciso*. As in the two works discussed
above, one is caught immediately by the attractiveness of the
opening idea and its simple but effective presentation, as well as
by the composer's ability to preserve the freshness of his material
by avoiding unnecessary repetition and by circling around its

tonality. Yet the success with which the main key of G minor has
been implanted can be appreciated when it is later recapitulated.
That the first movement is built on sonata principles is clear from
the balance of themes, its tonal processes, and not least from its
sense of movement. Within this discipline Stevens has a way of
metamorphosing his themes without undermining their identity,
perhaps offering a clue to the meaning of 'volubilmente' which
not only translates as 'volubly', (a word one would hesitate to use
to describe this music) but 'changeably' or 'inconstantly'.

The second movement is one of restrained melancholy with a
single moment of passion at its centre. A certain harmonic ambiguity adds tension to the music, which has a binary shape like a
condensed sonata form. The two main themes are strongly tonal.

But their accompanying harmonies (particularly in the case of
Ex.8 (a & b) are not what these melodies would lead us to expect.
The sense of harmonic uncertainty returns to add a question mark
to the final bars of the movement.

With the last movement we are back with Stevens the
contrapuntist who is, in any case, never far away. Basicly a
sonata design, the first subject is set out as a four-part fugal
exposition, with the interesting feature that each entry of the
subject is a minor third lower than the preceding one, allowing the
tonality to range more freely than a more orthodox tonic/dominant
procedure would do. The fugue subject, always accompanied by a
scale figure, sometimes *staccato*, sometimes *legato*, is characterised
by the interval of a fourth.

The same interval, inverted, starts the second subject a fanfare-like theme, barely harmonised, and heard first on violas.

Ex.10

There is little in the way of formal sonata-style development, but it can also be said that Stevens' music rarely stops developing, particularly when his forms are as compact as this. The recapitulation, for instance, takes the form of a double fugal exposition, first with the theme (and its accompanying scale) inverted, then again the right way up. A dramatic *pp subito poco a poco cresc.* takes us to a *ff Meno mosso* in which the second subject (Ex.10), now fully and richly harmonised, is used as the material for a final peroration in a no-nonsense G major.

The *Sinfonietta* was almost the last of his works that Stevens heard in a live performance, when the Prague Student Orchestra played it during their visit to Britain in 1982. He was intensely moved by the skill and commitment of the young musicians and by the conviction they brought to their performance. In a letter to Bertha Stevens after her husband's death Graham Whettam wrote:

> What I shall remember most vividly of him personally is the way his face seemed to light up with absolute joy when the Czech orchestra played his Sinfonietta last summer. I am so glad I was there.'

The reviewer for *Musical Opinion* wrote that 'A composer who can produce a movement [the *Adagio*] of this sustained quality is nowadays, alas, all too rare'.

The *Introduction, Variations and Fugue on a Theme of Giles Farnaby* was completed in January 1972, and first performed later the same year by the Chamber Orchestra of the Royal College of Music under James Harvey Phillips, at whose request the work had been composed. The theme, *Giles Farnaby's Dreame* (Ex.11), is taken from that great collection of early 17th-century keyboard pieces, the Fitzwilliam Virginal Book.

Like all good variation themes, this one has a number of features which impress it on the memory in a variety of ways. To mention just three: the rhythmic shape of the tune (a), the shift from D to F major for its middle section (b), and the distinctive final cadence

common to so many 16th- and 17th-century pieces (c), together
providing a sequence of landmarks which help the listener to keep
in step with the varied theme. The theme itself is preceded by an
Introduction based upon its last few bars (d).

Instant recognisability is not, of course, an essential factor in
variation writing, nor is it necessarily always a desirable one. In
Variation 1, for instance, we are offered but a skeletal version of
the theme and in Variation 2 the theme appears backwards in
long notes (strings and horns alternating) with decorative running
quavers in the woodwind; but for the most part, Stevens retains
a perceptible association between the theme, or bits of it, and the
variations. These are linked so skilfully that one is not aware of the
sectional nature of the form but rather of a continuously developing
exploration of its subject's potential. This sense of continuity is
enhanced by a constant tempo relationship between the first six
variations and the crotchet = 96 of the theme. Only with the sixth
variation 'Tempo di Siciliano' does the general impetus relax.

The *Adagio* seventh and eighth variations together form the
expressive centre of the work, with the thematic material extended
and developed with resourceful simplicity.

The Introduction which originally led to the theme now returns
to herald a Fugue – no extended movement this (as fugues following variations sometimes are) but a compact peroration which takes
up each phrase of the theme in turn, and develops it contrapuntally
in the manner of a chorale-prelude.

Stevens cannot have been unaware of the danger of anachronism
when early music is arranged for modern orchestra, and his instrumental colouring of the theme and the cadence (c) turns to good
account what could not be avoided. Throughout the piece, in fact,
the scoring is deft, colourful and transparent and, in keeping with
the work's provenance, clearly and successfully designed to exploit

the particular qualities of the different sections of the orchestra and allow them to shine. The orchestration is for pairs of flutes, oboes, clarinets, bassoons, horns and trumpets, three timpani and strings.

On their European tour in the Spring of 1972 the Royal College of Music Chamber Orchestra included the *Farnaby Variations*. The critic of the *Berner Tageblatt* wrote that 'Bernard Stevens' composition enchants not only through its artistic technique of composition but also by its extremely delicate sense of timbre'. Also in the audience was the violinist Max Rostal, for whom Stevens wrote his Violin Concerto, and who made his home in Bern after 25 years of living in Britain; he wrote to the composer: 'I was naturally very curious indeed to see which way you were going, since I have known several works of yours of an earlier period. I was very impressed with the mastery of invention, extremely clear form and brilliant orchestration; in other words, I really enjoyed your work! Congratulations!'

The cottage at Great Maplestead with the forge – the studio – beyond.
(From a line and wash sketch by Thomas Pitfield)

Bernard in the cottage garden with daughter Catherine dazzled
by the sun. 1953.

8
Orchestral Works
Edwin Roxburgh

My most vivid experience of Bernard Stevens' music was the performance of his Symphony No.2 by students of the Royal College of Music under Stephen Savage on 22 March 1979. The concert was in celebration of the tenth anniversary of the College's Twentieth Century Ensemble, which we had established in 1969. The function of the Ensemble is the study and performance of the avant-garde. To associate Stevens' music with this genre must seem strange in view of the intense traditionalism of his own style. It is not so strange if account is taken of the profound objectivity in his pronouncements about twentieth century music. He considered style to be subordinate to content when he said in an interview, 'I'm more interested in what I say than how I say it'. Other statements in the same interview intensify this point: 'I make it my business to become acquainted with every big new work, with every composer, then I decide in my own experience what is the value of it. I'm not hostile to avant-garde music in principle. All I ask is that a composer finds a language in which he can best say what he wants to say.'

It was this breadth of intellectual response to all music that made Stevens a champion of any organisation that sponsored new music. His support and help in promoting it at the R.C.M. was selfless and whole-hearted. Such characteristics coloured everything in his life. The performance of the Second Symphony was a tribute to his association with the Ensemble's work, as well as an acknowledgement of the broad spectrum of musical interests which preoccupied him.

Radical and outspoken, Stevens was also receptive to the views of friends who did not share his political and philosophical convictions. His philosophy embraced quite divergent elements. On the one hand he was a Marxist; on the other, he was a member of the Teilhard de Chardin Society. The balance he sought between the rational and the spiritual formed the essence of his sensibility, often becoming a motivating factor in his music. This is especially evident in his first symphonic work, *A Symphony of Liberation*, opus 7.

This work was composed between 1940 and 1945, much of which time the composer was in the Army. It won first prize in the *Daily Express* Victory Symphony Contest, which was judged by Sir Malcolm Sargent, Sir Arthur Bliss and Constant Lambert. The three movements recall the events of the war, and are appropriately called *Enslavement*, *Resistance* and *Liberation*. These characteristics also define the spirit of man and (in the composer's words) 'the dialectical process'. The work was dedicated to the memory of Clive Branson (a poet and painter) who was killed on the Arakan Front in 1944. Stevens once said that while he was working on the symphony his mind was filled with the heroic image of Branson. The first performance was given by the London Philharmonic Orchestra under Sargent in the Royal Albert Hall on 7 June 1946.

The experience of enslavement is evoked in a continuous slow melody throughout the first movement. Set against a melodic bass line, this travels with restraint, at first building slowly and gradually with tremendous control towards the climax near the end. A continuous chain of melody, built on the first three notes of the minor scale and hinged by shifting triads, creates a moving impression of an unyielding spirit locked in bondage. It carries a similar image of enslavement to that envisaged in *The Prisoners* by Michelangelo in the Galleria dell' Accademia in Florence, portraying straining torsos locked in stone blocks.

The influence of Vaughan Williams is apparent in the harmonic structure, which continually uses triadic relationships based on the main melodic interval of a minor third. The climax is a good example of this, showing the oscillation of A minor and C minor, not unlike the axis relationship which Bartók used. Taking A as the diminished fifth centre of the E flat octave (the tonic of the movement) and as the horizontal axis of Bartók's system, this climax represents the organic centre of the movement's harmonic structure. The sense of yearning is achieved at the very beginning of the movement when the subdominant is heard in the bass with a final resolution on to E flat only at the close. The *piano* coda, far from evoking resignation, seeks bitonal conflicts as an anticipation of the second movement, entitled *Resistance*. The subtitle 'Scherzo' applies to the spirit rather than the form. It is a phrenetic and energetic display of biting rhythmic motifs, demonstrating a release from the sustained passion of the first movement. The theme is based on the horizontal axis of G and C sharp, the first notes in the bass:

The first sequential passage relies on this relationship entirely, making several transitions to a powerful theme on a pedal D (the dominant), which is the episode. The three-note minor scale motif appears again here, as a bass accompaniment to the second motif of the episode. A relentless path is followed, leading to a defiant statement on the horns, disavowing the minor scale motif in a descending whole-tone scale based on major thirds. This leads back to the main theme in the tonic, followed by an augmentation in the bass and a huge climax on the third of the minor scale. The integration of this material is woven superbly into dramatic counterpoint throughout and, like the first movement, the Scherzo sustains an unchanging character.

The final movement presents the scale motif again in a solemn *fugato* opening in B minor:

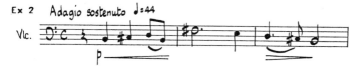

The accumulating thematic material based on this is the turning point in the work, when the *Allegro maestoso* changes it into a major third motif in B major:

In this movement, as in the others, there is a relentless quality about the development of the material. Through constant transitions and imitations the density of the counterpoint builds up towards the final resolution of the movement in a glorious B flat major. A sustained tonic pedal carries the coda to a pause – strangely, on the only dominant seventh in the piece; then the triumphal cadence emerges.

It is the quality of understatement and craftmanship in Stevens' music that appeals most. Indulgence has no place in the easy sincerity of his language. As Contant Lambert said of the work in his competition report: 'Not merely a glorification piece full of clichés: it has great emotional stress, handled with skill'. Sargent pinpointed a characteristic in the music which was prophetic: 'It has a poignancy and great emotional sincerity'. The two last words say a great deal about Stevens the man, and his musical development in years to come.

The allusion to Bartók is by no means fortuitous. Stevens loved his music. In conversation with me during his last illness he talked enthusiastically about Ernö Lendvai's analytical book on Bartók. The author explains the geometry of the music, with reference to the axis principle which he invented to establish a unique system of key relationships governing the harmonic structure of the music. Added to this he demonstrates the function of the Golden Section, the Fibonacci Series, and many other proportional devices used in Bartók's music. In hindsight it would have been important to know if the axis relationships I have explained in the *Liberation Symphony* were a conscious process for Stevens, but I failed to ask the question. It seems to me quite probable that he *was* aware of this, because it would be consistent with his thoughts on form and design. The adoption of techniques established by other twentieth century composers was by no means a magpie characteristic in him. He enjoyed such a shared identity in a very scholarly way. For instance, the second movement of his Second Symphony uses Messiaen's *Modes of Limited Transposition* quite unselfconsciously and with a completely distinctive identity.

In our conversation Stevens remarked that one issue which Lendvai had not discussed in depth was Bartók's concern for the timing of each section of a movement, which he took trouble to place in his scores. The temporal aspect of music was of great importance to form in Stevens' estimation. As in all his works, the *Liberation Symphony* shows this concern for proportion. The resulting sense of continuity is impressive and demonstrates the unquestionable influence of Bartók.

Fugal Overture

The title of his *Fugal Overture* opus 9 of 1947 is an obvious indication that the polyphonic characteristic was becoming intensified in Stevens' music. Clarence Raybould, who conducted one performance, wrote to the composer with a comment which illustrates this well: 'What a joy it is when one comes across a piece of music having such excellent craftmanship!' Using the same conventional orchestral forces as the *Liberation Symphony*, the work is woven around an intensely rhythmic subject:

In the score which Sargent used to conduct the BBC Symphony Orchestra performance at the Proms in 1948, he has written at the head of the subject in Ex. 4 'presumably *a tre battute*'. He inserted thick barlines at the point where I have marked crosses, making the first bar an anacrusis. Sargent seemed to make a habit of such bar grouping. My own view is that this device can sometimes work against the composer's rhythmic intentions, as it does in this work. To interpret the first bar as an upbeat to a $^9/_8$ group gives the barline an accentual significance which defies the asymmetrical nature of the rhythm by placing a stress on bar 5, thus defying the musical intention of the *crescendo*. Likewise, a rhythmic imitation of bars 8 and 10 is destroyed if bar 10 becomes the third beat of a $^9/_8$ group. Also the Subject ends in the thirteenth bar, overlapping the Answer, a clear indication of the suppleness of rhythm woven into the subject. Stevens intended 'one in a bar', with intermittent accents, to create a flexible rhythmic structure.

The 'excellent craftmanship' which Raybould refers to is an appropriate compliment, because the work demonstrates the

flowing counterpoint so characteristic of Stevens' technique. The
Subject and its working are subtle, but not as inspired as so much
of the *Liberation Symphony*. The desire to invent adventurous
material is always apparent, but the need to restrain and establish
boundaries prevented Stevens from altogether taking wing in this
work. Whereas Bartók achieves asymmetry in *Music for Strings,
Percussion and Celesta* with a fugue subject that contains four
different time signatures, and spans the ring of twelve fifths in its
harmonic structure, Stevens is unwilling to break the bounds of the
regular barline. With academic purity he limits his key structure to
the traditional tonic and dominant relationships in the exposition.
Exploration begins in the episode that follows. The arrangement
of modulations is often intriguing, as in the following example:

B flat minor modulates to B major by making G flat into an
enharmonic relationship with F sharp (bar 4 in Ex. 5). The parallel
chords which colour the middle entry bring us back to the E flat
major tonic with a sudden interruption to the brass episode, leading
the way to an interesting restatement in the final section, where the
subject is heard again in the tonic, but this time only in intervallic
outline, the repeated notes being allotted to an *ostinato* pedal on
the *pizzicato* double bass. The accumulation of material relies on
the scale figurations of the counter-subject, which is interrupted
by a pause before the brass enters with a variation of the opening
Maestoso, bringing the work to a grand close.

Compared to the *Liberation Symphony*, it is a modest work which
allows full rein to Stevens' contrapuntal skill. It has an athletic
quality which can be heard in many of the fast movements of the
other works.

Overture; East and West
Stevens' involvement in the Workers' Music Association led to a

number of songs and chorus settings. The years between 1947 and 1956 include eleven works connected with the Association, which demonstrate his concern for music for the working class. In 1950 he composed a work for the WMA Orchestra, an overture called *East and West* for Wind Band. It is a light-weight piece which can happily carry the tag of being 'occasional'*. 'East' is represented by the Russian folk song *In the field there stands a birch-tree*, which Tchaikovsky used in his Fourth Symphony. 'West' is revealed in *Greensleeves*. There is plenty of contrapuntal weaving. In spite of the deliberate simplicity of the material, Stevens manages to achieve an ingenious combination of both themes at the close with some nicely wrought invertible counterpoint. There is audacity in the choice of such standard material, but the craftsmanship brings a freshness to its unpretentious intentions. The idea of East and West joining hands in a rendering of national folk songs demonstrates Stevens' view that art is a universal language, and that part of its function is to stimulate the union of minds. In this way his socialism was manifested in all his music, together with a deep sense of love for humanity.

Dance Suite

In contrast, the *Dance Suite* opus 28 of 1957 is a work of stature. There is no doubt that here the inspiration comes from Bartók, even to the title. Like Bartók, Stevens uses the characteristic of folk music, but the material is entirely original and happily avoids even a hint of pastiche. In this work Stevens achieves something of his quest for a synthesis of convention and invention. The notion that music requires familiar landmarks is evident in all his work, but here it becomes a *raison d'être* for the composition. For instance, the first movement is a $9/8$ gig, based on traditional compound triplet figurations; but the character of the music is intense and dramatic. The element of economy and understatement requires compensation in the performance of music of this genre. (Edmund Rubbra, to whom the work is dedicated, belongs to the same school.) At the opening another traditional side-glance comes from the rhythmic displacement of hemiolas in the first four bars. After this, the octave couplings of the two-part writing give the lie

*It was written for a large celebration in the Empress Hall of the 33rd anniversary of the Soviet Union, organised by the British–Soviet Friendship Society; Stevens conducted its performance.

to the tonal ambiguity of the first movement. This desire to search for far-reaching relationships, which defy the tonal centre without destroying it, becomes an increasingly strong characteristic in the harmonic structure of Stevens' music as time progresses. The first movement begins with a D tonic, but closes on what is really A flat minor, the Bartók axis relationship. This is also reflected in the modal structure of the thematic material, which is based on the second of Messiaen's *Modes of Limited Transposition*:

The bracketed interval in Ex. 6 shows that the axis relationship is inherent in the mode, and establishes an organic link between the thematic substance and the harmonic structure. This can be seen clearly in the first theme, which starts on the seventh note of the eight-note mode:

I was able to discover one wrong note in the movement for the simple reason that it was the only note that did not conform to the mode! The extraordinary element of still life which is captured in the movement results from its confinement to only one transposition of the mode (a characteristically rational idea). This creates the relentless drive towards the explosive cadence, which was misunderstood in the first performance.

It seems that, once the decision to use this mode had been made, Stevens was unwilling to allow any deviation. Consistency was imperative for him in all matters. He could be a formidable opponent or a whole-hearted supporter; either way his judgment was unflinching and absolute.

The second movement takes the form of a passacaglia. The time signature is ⁵/₄ and, like Bach's *C minor Passacaglia and Fugue* for organ and Purcell's *Dido's Lament*, the bass has the same rhythmic structure in each bar until the cadence.

The relationship with the first movement can be seen in the D–G sharp tritone of the harmonic axis, and the persistent semitone

Ex 8   Andante ♩=66

resolution after each of these progressions. The familiar asymmetry of the seven-bar subject achieves the contemplative nature of the movement. The sombre opening builds to an impassioned climax with an *accelerando*. When this subsides into the original tempo on a D pedal-point in Variation II it is only to prepare for the true height of emotional intensity. This is achieved by disruption of the regular bars into fragments after an interpolated bar on the pedal, having the effect of delaying the climax in a very dramatic way. The tuba then takes up the passacaglia below a brass statement, before the subdued eleven-bar coda.

The *Allegretto* ²/₂ tempo and time-signature of the third movement seem to indicate a Pavane. The prominence of the harp against an oboe melody indicates the grace of this dance, although Stevens does not specify titles in any of the movements. Like the previous one, this is anchored to a tonic throughout, this time on E with an ambivalent third, G sharp/A flat, hingeing the chromatic diversions. Like Bartók, Stevens could rarely resist the temptation of an inversion, and we discover the oboe theme upside down in the cellos within a few bars. This movement acts as gentle episode before the exertions of the fourth, which defies the connotation of a traditional dance because it is in ¹¹/₈ time. The five main beats, with an extended triplet at the end of each bar, are very much in the *Portsmouth Point* tradition, while achieving the very personal, lithe quality of Stevens' livelier music. The cellos and basses introduce the main tonic-dominant motif, B flat to F, immediately after the short brass introduction:

Ex 9   Presto ♩=152

The melodic elements presented above this are continually syncopated, so that the dance is revealed as something of a revel:

The whirling effect is achieved by constant statements and inversions of three-note groups, which sometimes become regular in interpolated $^6/_8$ bars. The constant shift of accent is occasionally interrupted by emphatic $^4/_4$ bars. The arch-contrapuntist enters when the main theme (Ex. 10) arrives augmented as an ingenious canon in the trombones and tuba:

Ingenious, because the theme has been in $^{11}/_8$; the canon begins on the second beat of the bar, and its second voice enters on the second beat of the second bar, so that the accentuation in this augmented version transforms the material. It is an ideal use of canon, which emulates Bach in its disguising of the technique involved, by employing figurative ingenuity. This happens in three consecutive statements in the brass, set against the tonic-dominant motif with energetic display in the rest of the orchestra. Sequential development of this material becomes an episode of mounting activity until the coda, when the canons in the brass present the main thematic material augmented in emphatic statements. This establishes a return to the B flat tonic, concluding the work in triumphant spirit.

Looking through the score of this work the reader will find evidence that Stevens always writes well within the technical capabilities of the performers. The instruments are never required to rise or fall beyond their comfortable range, and no exotic or exceptional effects are demanded. There is some affinity with Lennox Berkeley in this, which reminds me of a statement which that composer made about his own music. He described it as 'connoisseur's music'. I find that description totally apposite to Bernard Stevens: 'I'm more interested in what I say than how I say it'. What he wanted to say was always honest and unpretentious, in his life and in his music. He was never demanding in his approach to others, and made a point of encouraging people to be themselves, honestly and unpretentiously. This quality certainly attached to his teaching, and made him a much-loved man among his students, colleagues and friends. Overstatement was foreign to Stevens' nature. (He disliked the 'long high note' habit in opera, and showed this clearly in *The Shadow of the Glen*.) Therefore, his orchestration remained modest in its demands on the musicians for the same reason. It is the craftsmanship of the counterpoint and structure which appeals in the *Dance Suite*. The immediate impact of the sound is judged with precise aural perception.

Prelude and Finale

His skill for writing effectively within the bounds of conventional capabilities made Stevens the most adaptable of composers. This is proved in opus 31b, his *Prelude and Finale* for orchestra, which was composed for a series published from 1960 by Novello, called *Music for Today*. This consisted of new orchestral works composed expressly for amateurs, edited by Geoffrey Bush, whose foreword explains its nature: 'The aim . . . is to introduce amateur orchestral players (of all ages) to the work of serious contemporary composers. The only limitations imposed on contributors have been technical ones; each piece has been kept within the capacity of keen amateur players, but otherwise there are no compromises, concessions, or "writing-down" of any sort'. The danger in such an enterprise was the same as in certain schools concerts of that period, which aimed at easy accessibility and response for young audiences, but often ended up by being patronising. Bush could not have chosen a better composer than Stevens for such a task. The decision to compose a conventional fugue might not have been the most inspired idea, because it did not introduce the amateurs to the experimental and avant-garde pursuits of that period. But Stevens was totally aware

of this, and did not bend towards any language in which he did
not speak freely and honestly. Accepting this, the work is finely
wrought and presents an impressive display of the composer's
skill. It was first performed by the then Northern School of Music
Orchestra under Meredith Davies in 1962.

The short Prelude is based on motifs that appear later in the
Fugue. Stevens' allegiance to Vaughan Williams is evident in the
consecutive triads, which create a transient dissonance throughout
the imitative phrases of this opening statement. G major is never far
away, being clearly established in the first statement of the Fugue
subject:

Ex 12

A very positive point is made in choosing a four-part fugue, in
that any weak elements in the amateur orchestra can be covered by
alternative instruments, which are carefully cued by the composer.
It also provides scope for doubling the 'voices' with various
combinations of instruments to produce a colourful orchestration.
The exposition is completed with two redundant statements when
all parts are active, leading to an episode derived from the subject.
Rather than a middle entry, a march 'interlude' takes over. It is the
beginning of the final section, which takes the form of an inversion
of the subject in the relative minor, set against jabbing E minor
chords. It leads to the final entry with a return to the tonic. The
coda builds towards the climax with a change to $^2/_4$ (dotted crotchet
= crotchet). This effectively halts the flow of counterpoint, and
brings the piece to a close on a sustained tonic pedal.

Prelude and Finale was originally composed as a work for Wind
Band entitled *Adagio and Fugue*, opus 31a. In some ways this is the
more effective version. The variety of colours and timbres enhances
the clarity of the 'voices' in the fugue, giving a remarkable range
of sonorities and textural variation to the piece. It deserves to be
high on the repertoire list of any wind band. In two places the

material differs from that of the orchestral version. The central interlude is replaced by a short section of *stretti* and $^3/_4$ statements of the subject, augmented against a pedal point in the timpani; the coda retains $^3/_4$ instead of going into $^2/_4$. The final tonic pedal remains.

Symphony no. 2 opus 35

After the initial success of the *Symphony of Liberation* Stevens pursued a wide variety of forms in his compositions, but it was eighteen years before he tackled another symphony. During this time his style of composing developed a more controlled and organic approach. By 1964, when he completed his *Second Symphony*, the world of the avant-garde was separated widely from the traditionalists. The former considered the symphony to be dead, while the latter insisted on its imperishable aspects. The nature of the problem rested in the fact that the symphony, like the concerto and sonata, originally depended on tonal key relationships for the elements of its structure. In atonal music intervals are not married to a tonal centre, so that the marriage of two concepts created a question for those who had renounced tonal principles. The fact that Schönberg was able to compose a masterpiece in the *Wind Quintet* (his first twelve-note work), using classical forms and moulding them into atonal music, is the kind of mystery that forms the essence of a great artist. In principle, it seems impossible. Today the question seems to have been answered to some extent, and the symphony has been revitalised by the debate, not because the relationships of form and idiom are now resolved in this matter, but because the nature of the symphony, together with other classical forms, has emerged with other characteristics.

As a traditionalist, Stevens remained a tonal composer all his life, so that his music was undisturbed by the questions posed by atonality. This does not mean that he was unconcerned or uninterested in the avant-garde. On the contrary, the very nature of my friendship with him centred on intense discussions about all that was new, all of which, he insisted, had been done before. We spent many hours disagreeing on such issues, except when a true masterpiece arose which transcended all factionalism and found us on a similar wave-length. An example of our differences on this issue can be quoted from his interview published in the WMA Bulletin no.4, 1983: 'I cannot see the point in a composer not writing in a way

that is comprehensible to the greatest number of people'. If I were
to reply: 'Who is to decide what are the criteria for such a musical
language?' the debate would become philosophical, and a tough
defence would have to be made against a mind that romped through
politics, history, philosophy and literature with immense authority.
Nevertheless, it was characteristic of him that he masterminded a
festival of avant-garde music at London University in 1976 with
great relish and excitement, during a period when he had very little
time to compose for five years because of his joint commitment at
the University and the R.C.M.

This absence of conflict in his idiom gave a freedom to
his writing that made symphonic form an easy vessel to fill,
which could continue where Sibelius had left it in his Seventh
Symphony. The motivic tapestry which served the Finn was by
no means an exhausted form in Stevens' eyes. The performance of
Stevens' Second Symphony at the R.C.M. in March 1979 proved
its freshness and durability fifteen years after its composition.

Although the contrapuntal element is as strong here as elsewhere
in the composer's output, it is built on related thematic motifs in
the manner of Sibelius. The sustained development of the first
movement of this work is intensified in manner and achieves
a concentrated interplay of imitation. Like Sibelius it relies on
repetition, sustaining incessant and subtle transformation, so that
nothing is heard as a statement for revival in a recapitulation. Nor
indeed is there an exposition, because the movement is a set of
linked variations based on a twelve-note theme:

Ex 13

Of course, the style does not derive from Schönberg, any more
than it did for Walton in the twelve-note motif of his Second
Symphony. The triadic harmonies are derived from the theme and
based on entirely tonal principles. The movement is shaped by a
line of rising *tempi* which govern the transformation of the material
from a dark, sinewy opening, gathering in vigour and finding its
climax at a point near the close, where the torrent of the *accelerando*
ceases and meets an open sea in a brass pronouncement of the
transformed main material. It is as if you hear this true subject

for the first time at the close. Everything foreshadows this single statement. Example 14 shows the principal motifs derived from the row:

Motifs (a) and (b) are directly related, but (c) acts as a counter-subject to material derived from (a) and (b). The rising semitone of the anacrusis in (a) and (b) is a prominant feature of the whole movement, giving a sense of urgency to its development. The vaguest shadow of the sonata principle is evident as the transformations continue around the interplay of figurations, Ex 14 representing the first group of elements. Ex 15 shows the second group:

The *accelerando* is evident throughout Exs. 14 and 15. Stevens' love of modes is shown here in the Phrygian intervals of Ex. 14(a). The 'dying fall' of the Phrygian cadence, created by the first semitone of the mode being next to the tonic, gives the sense of tonal ambience so characteristic of this composer. The melodic reflection of this can be seen in the semitones of Ex. 14(a), and (b), and 15(a) and (b).

An episodic variation based on an *ostinato* acts as a short development. It is here as a further step towards the true exposition of the material at the close. Ex. 16 shows the *ostinato* in the bass as a counter-subject to the melodic motif, derived from example 14(a). Note the metronome marking, which is twice as fast as in Ex 13:

The semitone figure is featured in the clarinet motif, Ex 16(b), which is developed throughout the *ostinato*, which itself becomes transformed and is stemmed by a G.P. bar which announces the final rush (now crotchet 192) into the final slow variation in G minor. Another G.P. bar reduces the speed again, making the smooth sea that has been reached into a calm reflection of all that has been experienced. Although the movement finishes in G minor, an ambivalence remains with a final *pizzicato* D in the cellos and double basses.

In a letter to Stevens, Edmund Rubbra says: 'The movement that made an immediate impact was the Scherzo, and the seemingly "circular" form was so naturally achieved when the initial trills returned at the end'. This second movement is certainly compelling, and seems wholly characteristic of Stevens at his best. The fact that he jumps from Schönberg's twelve-note motivation to Messiaen's *Modes of Limited Transposition* is neither here nor there. The deployment of either element did not affect the personal character of the music, which comes through as entirely his own.

The basic idea behind the movement is an attempt to apply some of the principles of physical movement developed by Rudolph Laban, the Slovak choreographer, who was with the Berlin State Opera in the 1930s. Strong quick movements represented in the opening section contrast with the sustained but flexible actions which motivate the Trio. This is dominated by invertible canons in the brass. These sections are linked by free, cadenza-like passages for the woodwind, which consistently use the Modes of Limited Transposition without the faintest hint of stylistic inconsistency.

In the introduction, the oscillation between two notes, E and C sharp (derived from the mode), is a link between the beginning and the end, reflecting Rubbra's comment; the movement starts on C sharp and ends on E. The falling minor third is reflected in all the material. An example can be seen in the second motif on the horns in E, which is repeated later by the strings in C sharp. In this way the harmonic and melodic material enjoy a happy union which is evident in the sheer joy that is projected.

The third movement acts as a slow introduction to the fourth. It is a sustained Canzona based on a twelve-note theme:

Ex 17

The progressions from the second note onwards are identical to those in the row of the first movement, as shown in Ex 13. Schönberg's technique is not employed in all elements of the organic structure, but a strong allusion to the 'fourths motif' of the Viennese composer's *Kammersymphonie* is made in the first three notes of the row. This material is introduced as a fugal exposition before the Canzona develops. It is characteristic of Stevens that all the instruments share the Canzona substance in a flowing, contrapuntal web. Trochaic figurations on the brass build up tension against broad statements of the fourths motif, until a new figure appears which becomes the main theme of the Finale. With a quickening tempo and an *accelerando* the seams of the movements are sewn imperceptibly – an ingenious metamorphosis.

The Finale is a Rondo. Episodes are clearly defined by changes of time from ³/₄ to ³/₂ and ²/₄. There is real fire in the opening statement of the main theme on the horns and violas:

Ex 18

Although the movement is founded on G minor, this subject demonstrates the flexibility of the key relationships throughout the movement. The first two bars establish G minor; then the subject moves through D flat major, C flat major and G flat major before unexpectedly returning to the initial supertonic of G minor. Things are not really settled tonally, so that when the final G major chord resounds it is an absolute in terms of form, in that the piece cannot go beyond this point. It is an ideal conclusion, patterned from the material of the entire movement. The first episode contrives to begin in A flat major, eventually stating the episode motif augmented in the tonic, forming a Stevensian brass interlude of elegant dynamism. This is transformed into a compressed development in ²/₄, drawing in the middle statement of the Rondo en route. The counterpoint shows Stevens at his best, for while the Rondo material is being developed, the trombones and tuba state the slow movement twelve-note theme with impressive majesty. When the horns enter, this is compounded by canonic statements which lead to the sort of climax that might induce other composers to indulge in histrionics. For Stevens, this is out of the question. It is short-lived, and goes on to the final section with yet another build-up of contrapuntal intensity, which includes a reappearance in augmentation of the Canzona theme of the slow movement. The coda in C is reached with glorious conclusiveness.

To place this work in the context of the time when it was composed makes it an outstanding statement of individualism. I am not sure why Stevens felt it necessary to use elements of atonal techniques without committing them to the musical functions for which they were designed. There is no question about the non-organic function of them in his music, and he would not have pretended otherwise. He once defended his approach in conversation with me by quoting Frank Martin as an example of such use of the row, making his point by clearly associating himself with such a precedent. The integration of the thematic material derived from the row is certainly consistent in style, and has the touch of the sensitive artist behind all Stevens' work. The result is a major achievement and an important contribution to the symphonic repertoire.

Variations for Orchestra

In my opinion the next orchestral work shows a lull in Stevens'
inspiration. It is the *Variations for Orchestra*, opus 36, composed
in 1964. The composer is careful to avoid the word 'Theme' in
the title. As Ex 19 demonstrates, there is no specific theme:

The material is made up of the contrapuntal, imitative phrases which form the basis of so much of Stevens' music. It gives the impression of being an introduction. Variation 1 is, in fact, more clearly the foundation for the opening variations, which are very free, and joined imperceptibly, even to the point of overlapping at times. This disguise of the basic material is skilfully achieved, but the material is not very substantial. Ex 20 shows the passacaglia bass of Variation 1, which is repeated four times, as upper parts enter one by one in the strings:

Bars 4 and 5 show the foundation of the material to be based on the Locrian mode without the initial semitone interval. This features predominantly in the bracketed intervals of Ex 19. The problem here seems to be that none of the material contains figurative features, so that the whole work relies too much on the crotchet unit. This is an extremely difficult proposition, especially in the first seven variations, which are very slow and ponderous. It is the Locrian semitone which invites most interest. Ex 19 shows the foundation key to be E flat minor, and the close of the work in E flat major confirms this. But the D in the bass reiterates the semitone conflict that features throughout the work.

The intervallic relationships which form the melodic substance for all the variations are reflected in each of the voices in Example 19. In the top voice the rising fourth motif finds its reflection in the falling D—A of the bass, as does the minor third in bars 14—15. Bars 6—8 in the top voice are a retrograde version of 1—2, with the significant semitone added at the end. The same feature is shown in bars 9—11. But in the next bar, the upper voice becomes the reflection of the inner, using its opening five notes in an augmented version from bars 12—17, making it the dominating interval of the work. Its constant appearance in the inner voice is the key to the elegiac character of the opening variations, which feature the passacaglia motif of Ex 20 continuously.

Closer examination shows that the relationships go deeper than this, for the first two bars of Ex 19 reveal a tone row shared by all the three parts. Bars 6—8 are a retrograde version. The first violins present it in a single-line melody in Variation 1, and the oboe plays the retrograde in Variation 2. By dividing the row between all the voices the material for melodic development in the variations remains hidden at the outset, making the opening material effectively an introduction, the revealed melodic substance appearing only in Variation 11. This is a subtle turn to the traditional form.

Variation 8, *Allegro*, changes the mood abruptly, adhering closely to the basic material of Ex. 19 in diminished form. The rather predictable inversion of this material appears in Variation 9, and inverted canonic versions in Variations 10 and 11. Invertible counterpoint, including canons, makes up the characteristic brass interlude of Variation 12, which reaches climactic proportions for full orchestra in Variation 13. And so the contrapuntal weaving of the material continues through the subsequent numbers, with E flat minor predominating until Variation 27 where, at the close, a violin solo reduces the material to two-voice proportions with the upper voices of bars 1 and 2 in Ex 19. Variation 28 exposes the row in a clear statement from the lower strings, set against a sustained D in the horns, reverting to the *Andante* tempo of Variation 1. This becomes a melody in the clarinet, which sustains the movement as a calm interlude before the *Allegro* coda variations. The tuba, double-bassoon and double-bass intrude on this current of polyphony in Variation 32 with a subdued statement of the complete row. The rest of the brass continue similar motifs in Variation 33, leading to the final variation on a sustained E flat. The trumpets call out the main upper motif of the opening against a canonic inversion in the low brass, culminating on a resounding E flat chord, which seems inexplicable in the note-row context. It is as if Stevens was acknowledging the mastery of Schönberg's music, which he certainly admired, but ultimately defying his own flirtation with the tone-row technique. 'The singer, not the song' seems to speak through this gesture, and exposes the uncertainty which pervades the Variations. It is of course an uncertainty born of integrity. Stevens was constantly questioning, reappraising and, indeed, discovering. The change in his political allegiances which came about as a result of the Russian occupation of Hungary in

1956 is a measure of his rational approach to any matter. For him all aspects of life and thought had to remain open to discovery and research and, like all good philosophers, he would occasionally doubt his own conclusions. Apart from the short *Nocturne on a Note-row of Ronald Stevenson* opus 51, the row was put aside after the Variations.

Stevens' orchestral language, being based on a linear, contra-puntal technique of composition, relied very much upon octave doubling of the individual voices of the counterpoint. For this reason the twelve-note language was incompatible with his motivations. Although I have not illustrated it in Ex 19, all the voices are doubled in octaves, which belies its twelve-note intentions. These technical contradictions work against the ideas, and are ill-at-ease with the manner. The fact that Stevens was compelled to experiment with a technique foreign to his own stylistic syntax is a measure of the intellectual force behind his quest for unification of impulse and technique. The empirical statement which resulted from this in the Variations proves the stylistic integrity and honesty of the man, in that such an adventure did not lead him away from his chosen path.

Choriamb
The quest did not retrieve the ring in the Variations, and we find Stevens very much at home again in his next orchestral composition, *Choriamb*, opus 41. Completed in 1968, this work was commissioned by the Harlow Festival for the Essex Youth Orchestra, which performed it with great success, and with his daughter as co-leader, in 1969; Graham Teacher conducted. With his usual skill for composing manageable parts to play, Stevens' gifts were aptly applied to the needs of young performers. Triadic harmonies are back, and the counterpoint ranges, with all the instruments thoroughly active and effective. The octave couplings find an essential role in the polyphony, and figurative details abounds.

A choriamb is a Greek metrical foot which Stevens defines as a type of rhythm in six. So the piece is in $^3/_2$. The rhythm of the first bar is ♩ ♩ ♩ ♩ It has many possibilities for cross-rhythm figures, which explains why the work has rhythmic buoyancy. Beyond this there is no attempt to imitate the sound of Ancient Greek music. The main thematic idea is heard at the opening. It is based on rising and falling fourths, together with semitones:

Ex 21 Adagio ♩=42

Brass

In the following *Allegro* this takes on a characteristic transformation
in shorter note-values, while the fluctuations of key implied by the
bracketed intervals carry the music through the constantly shifting
harmonies which are familiar from the earlier works, the fourths
and semitones abounding in all the figurations. A gradual increase
in tempo is reminiscent of the Second Symphony, but in such a
short piece the comparison can only be superficial.

Choriamb was the last of the large orchestral works, leaving only
the substantial cantata *Et Resurrexit*, opus 43, to be discussed. This
was commissioned by the Tilford Bach Festival Society, with the
assistance of Peter Morrison, and performed in the Festival under
Denys Darlow's baton. It is inscribed 'In Memoriam, Randall
Swingler'.

Six months before he died, I visited Stevens in hospital while he
was recovering from a state of coma. Although he was weak and
depressed, he wanted to talk about his life and friends. Swingler
touched a sensitive nerve and brought tears to his eyes. Their
friendship had been deep and inspiring for each of them. The
settings of Swingler's poetry in *The True Dark* and other works
are an indication of this, so that no explanation is needed for the
choice of this poet's work in association with the sacred text of
Ecclesiastes.

    I. (*Swingler*)
       Roll away the heavy stone!
       Let in the sharp light and wake the rocky dark!
       Look!
       Hark!
       Is there still flesh upon the bone?
       Is there still a pulse to tell
       The measure of heaven and hell?
       What kiss shall betray
       The lost life into fallible day?
       What breath re-start
       The silent heart?

BERNARD STEVENS

(*Ecclesiastes*: Ch.I.)
That which hath been
Is that which shall be:
And that which hath been done
Is that which shall be done
And there is no new thing
Under the sun.

II. (*Swingler*)
The dying eyes
Are fixed like violets
On a faith in a whole world
That will one day awake
To the wonder of its simple Being
They alone are seeing
In that last breathless moment.
This
The true resurrection
Is!

(*Ecclesiastes*: Ch.4.)
Out of prison
He came forth to be king:
Yea, even in his kingdom
He was born poor.
I saw all the living
That walk under the sun:
And they were with
The youth:

III. (*Ecclesiastes*: Ch.3.)
Who knoweth the spirit of man?
Whether it goeth upward?
And the spirit of the beast
Whether it goeth downward
To the earth?

(*Swingler*)
Glory, then, glory to the young leaf!
Glory no less to winter's tender grief
Which uncovers and waters
The hidden roots
Of longing and of love; and at last returns
Earth's dew-fresh daughter
From her Demetrian womb
To her new-found
Majestic paternal sun!

The fatalism of the first poem seems to indicate a belief that the persecution and slaughter of Christ is a symbol of what will continue to happen, and in the second poem, that death itself is the true resurrection. The quotations from *Ecclesiastes* are an expression of redemption through death.

In composing for an amateur chorus, and being conscious of limited rehearsal time, Stevens has kept the material essentially simple. The first of the four sections is centred on G minor and achieves a directness and clarity which make a virtue of simplicity. This is achieved effortlessly and without stylistic concessions. The contralto solo has most of the first poem to herself. Characterisation is achieved through balance of intervals rather than nuance or dramatic gesture, 'the sharp light' being painted by the simple expedient of a major seventh leap upwards. Although there are repeated figurations in the strings' accompaniment, the music sustains contrapuntal elements, leaving the voice single at all times, so that good balance is no problem in performance. The chorus is reserved for the more emphatic statements at the close, 'That which hath been—', where the voices, in Stevensian fashion, are doubled at the octave, sustaining a colourful doubling of the lower part at three octaves' distance in the flutes and bassoons.

The second movement is dominated by the chorus, with writing very similar to the first. Stevens sustains the connecting relationship of the two poems in this way, while using entirely new material based on rising and falling semitones. When the last line of the first stanza arrives, a startling contrast is made in a passage based on successive six-four chords, rising from F sharp major to E flat:

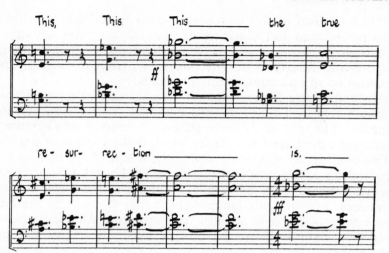

A slow ⁴/₄ marching bass, founded on minor thirds and semitones, with familiar inversions, sets the character of the tenor solo section, which has the same intervallic characteristics. The last line is echoed by the chorus, in the only florid chorus-writing that Stevens uses in the entire work. The significance in the six-four progressions is revealed on the last major six-four chord, which has a glow of brilliance characterising the resurrected Christ.

The third movement is an orchestral interlude which follows up the glorious chord in an exuberant Scherzo. This is a torrential *moto perpetuo* of a fugue, which seems like a breaking dam bursting the restraint of the counterpoint in the first two movements. It is a splendid movement, full of vigour, ingenuity and compelling intensity, created in the spirit of the great fugue in the *Alla Marcia* of Beethoven's Ninth Symphony. It is Stevens at his most inspired. In the process he contrives to make the movement into a sustained link between the brilliant ending of the second, and the chorus's powerful opening of the fourth. Here the Stevens' massed octaves serve to make the change of character for the archaic words of the biblical text. The simplicity of the first movement is recaptured. After the first phrase an echo of the ⁹/₈ Scherzo emerges, as if Stevens is unwilling to leave it behind. This dissolves into a sustained section with rising fourth motifs passing through the orchestra, which is a preparation for a sustained repetition of the word 'glory'. It is accompanied by rising scale figurations in the orchestra, which are a foretaste of their presentation at the close of the chorus. The rising fourths are then heard on 'glory' before the passage moves on. There is an effective piece of bitonality on the word 'womb': G major in the strings is set against C sharp major in the woodwind, reminding us of the mobility of the harmonic structure in Stevens' music.

In the last section the soloists and chorus join forces against rising cascades in the orchestra for the final reiterations of 'glory' in a tumultuous climax with, for once, an operatic top A in the tenor solo and, indeed, a high F for the basses! Rising from a sense of tragedy at the opening, the work closes in a stream of sunlight and optimism. It is a powerful and sensitive tribute to a great friend.

This is a work which any choral society would relish. It has the substance of undemanding gratification for the chorus and soloists, as well as immediate effectiveness with limited rehearsal time for the conductor and orchestral musicians. Stevens has composed here an accessible work which is wholly in keeping with his artistic integrity, and one which often reaches the heights of his achievements.

It is consistent with his nature that all Stevens' orchestral works demonstrate practicability as a dominant feature, not only in the undemanding technical characteristics, but in the orchestral forces as well. Most of the works use a minimum symphony orchestra complement, with very little use of percussion and extra instruments. However, the undemanding element of his orchestra is not only a matter of economy. The fact is that Stevens did not embrace exotic and colourful strokes in his composing technique. His preference was always for clearly drawn lines and explicit counterpoint. For this reason there is a great deal of octave and unison doubling in the writing which does not call for textural treatment. It is always bold and direct, as was the man.

At work in the studio.

Sharing a joke with pianists Mary Peppin and James Gibb and poet
Randall Swingler.

9

Music for Solo Piano
Ronald Stevenson

Theme and Variations op 2 (1941)

The theme is an *andante cantabile* in D flat in four-part texture with some octave-doubling, suggestive of organic 16-foot registration. The time signature $^3/_2$ $^2/_2$ relates to medieval prolation. The harmonic language is also Janus-headed, for it mixes modality with chromaticism. The theme's modulation-scheme encompasses D flat, C minor, E minor and back to D flat in its first eight bars; and the symmetrical inversion of that scheme in its second section of nine bars – F, G, E and F minor with a Neapolitan inflection – effects a return to D flat. This plan, consisting of modulation through unrelated keys, is an extension of one of Stevens' hallmarks: harmonic progression by unrelated chords; each harmony a familiar one, but rendered unfamiliar by juxtaposition. The first eight bars of the theme have the melody in the soprano, beginning in D flat. The second section of the theme has the melody in the bass, beginning in F.

Those two tonalities are telescoped in Variation 1; the bass beginning in F, the treble in D flat. The music is propelled by canon in syncopation against a background of quaver figuration in $^4/_4$ and in *allegro*, which is maintained for the first three variations.

Stevens' conception of variation form in this work does not follow the classical concept of adherence to the theme's tonality plan; rather does it select aspects of the theme for development.

Thus Variation 2 begins as a *basso ostinato* in F minor (the tonal centre of the theme's second section), in a motoric $^5/_4$. Here the modulation explores the tritone relationship which featured in Variation 1. In this way the work does not merely develop ideas from the theme but accumulatively develops ideas between the variations themselves.

Also, the length of the variations is constantly changed: a radical treatment of the form. Against the theme's seventeen bars, Variation 1 has thirteen, Variation 2 nine and Variation 3 seven bars. Thus the work contracts and expands in a vibrant, muscular manner, like a living organism.

Already in his opus 2 Stevens is a master. He has re-thought variation form. This work contains much to edify a young composer and to encourage new ways of refashioning old forms (variation being the most ancient of all forms, as it is found even in folk ballads).

Both Variations 3 and 4 are octave studies: no. 3 in inversion between the hands (the modulation-scheme being a condensation of the theme); no. 4 superimposing the polyrhythm of four beats against six, and the bitonality of A major in the bass against C sharp minor in the treble.

Variation 5 relaxes the tempo to *allegretto* and extends the time span to 31 bars, to enable a canon at the octave to develop at first in quavers, then in semiquavers, modulating freely from and to C sharp minor/major; and all kept *pianissimo*.

Variation 6 is a barcarolle-like *adagio* in $^{12}/_8$ with a *cantilena* and an inner counterpoint over an undulating ground bass. Only nine bars here, though it sounds longer because of the slow tempo. The tonality is rooted in C sharp, with side-glances at F minor and A minor/major.

Variation 7 is a *molto allegro* arpeggio study in inversions of hand-groups, modulating from and back to E minor in $^3/_4$.

Variation 8 is a neo-baroque, double-dotted, heroic *adagio*, mainly in octaves with some clangorous chords and the Locrian inflection of the tritone rooted on E, then on F.

The theme's tempo is re-established in $^3/_4$ in Variation 9, a bold *cantabile* inversion of the theme, transposed to A flat minor with widely spaced left hand arpeggi covering an octave with its upper tenth in a pianistic off-beat 'pizzicato'.

Variation 10 is an *allegro* canon at the 9th in octaves in ejaculated quaver phrases, with the tonality in flux.

Variation 11 is an *allegro molto* fugato-jig in three voices. An extended reiterated pedal-point affords a moment of relaxation from the surrounding free modulatory movement: another example of how everything is planned and balanced in his work, so that invention is varied and never flags, ensuring the listener's constant interest.

There is only the merest adumbration of the theme in the reiterated octave bass to Variation 12, which continues from the previous reiterated pedal point. This carrying over of texture between variations helps to make the form seamless, unlike the sectionalised 18th century variation form. Arpeggio figuration juts above the bass's broken octaves, as the tonality moves in and out of F major.

Variation 13 draws nearer to the theme in an another barcarolle-like (or nocturnal) *adagio* with a *cantilena* in the Dorian mode transposed to E minor, underpinned by lapping arpeggi in $^6/_8$. A lyrical moment in the work; a lovely page.

The *adagio* tempo is carried over into Variation 14, but the form is another canon with octave doublings, this time canon at the tritone. The recurrent canons at different intervals invoke the same procedure as in Bach's *Goldberg Variations*.

Variation 15 is a brief *andante* transition of eight bars in $^9/_8$ in three-part counterpoint, moving from and back to the tonal centre of F with only hints and snatches of the theme.

Variation 16 is an *allegretto* melody introduced by, and over, a wide-spanning arpeggio left hand: another nocturne-type. It begins on F and half-way through its 13 bars it veers to B – again the tritone-relationship.

Variation 17 is again closer to the theme's outline. Here the style of writing extends the late-period intermezzo-style Brahms: an intimate *andante con moto* with broken 10ths on off-beats, accompanying a melody in chords which adhere very closely to the ground plan of the theme's tonality, except that where the key was major in the theme, now it is minor, and vice versa.

The finale is an extended *passacaglia*, not on the theme but on its bass. Beginning *andante* in D flat, the note values decrease and the texture proliferates so that the tempo seems to increase, while remaining the same. Just before the end there is a *presto*, like a sudden resolve, then a big *ritardando* leads to a large, magistral close in the basic key of D flat. This work does something that very few composers were attempting in 1942: to reconcile baroque and romantic styles (exemplified in the recurrent canons and nocturnes); and yet the baroque can very well be considered in its plasticity and flamboyance of line as a pre-echo of romanticism.

It is observable that only on three mere beats of the work, on its last page, is the top octave of the piano touched. This indicates that there are no highlights, there is no glitter, nothing external about this sound world. Neither counterpoint nor harmony is delineated in the piano's top register: that is a determining factor. Stevens thus has much in common with the sound world of Brahms rather than Liszt. Remembering Schoenberg's characterisation of Brahms as a 'progressive', there is no need for this comparison to appear at all negatory of Stevens: on the contrary.

Another original (and therefore rare) feature is a vocabulary that extracts both clear, uncluttered contrapuntal lines *and* rich harmony. Few composers are masters of both.

Five Inventions op 14 (1950)

Counterpoint and harmony are juxtaposed here: Inventions 1, 3 and 5 are contrapuntal and quick; 2 and 4 are harmonic and slow; a simple scheme, effective in performance.

Again, one of the Stevens hallmarks of unrelated keys is found in the tonality ground plan. 1 is in G flat, 2 in A flat minor, 3 in E minor, 4 in G minor, 5 in F sharp minor/major. This tonal macrocosm is reflected in the microcosms of modulating within each piece: for instance, the first explores keys a third apart (if enharmonically) such as G flat and D; and the last piece juxtaposes the tonal centres of F sharp and B flat. In rapid succession, this procedure has the effect of sudden darkening and brightening of the tonal palette: the sonic equivalent of the visual impression of a field alternately lit with sunshine and shaded by cloud.

Writing in *Music Review* (May 1952) Hans Keller analysed the *Five Inventions* in elegant mathematical terms. He begins by opining that 'those miniatures are much more important than their size would seem to warrant'. Discovering the diminished seventh chord E, G, B flat and C sharp, underpinning the modulatory plan of Invention 3, he postulates a neat series of integers to represent its symmetrical exhaustion of tonal space. 'Starting from E (0) and progressing a minor third up (+) or down (−) every bar, the plan of the first 16 bars would be 0, +1, +2, +1, 0, −1, −2, −1, −2, −3, −2, −1, 0, +1, +2, +1, 0. When, at the entry of the middle-part (bar 17), not only the original *tune* is inverted but also the *harmonies*, which now move on *major* tonics in the opposite direction (i.e. 0, −1, −2, −1, 0, +1, etc.) − a considerable feat of skill if the return of A should be strict, as it is − then, at this moment, the ABA structure has become as over-determined as a right-angled isosceles triangle of which the hypotenuse were given in addition to the side.' Keller concludes his review like this: 'Stevens does not wholly succeed in solving the modern harmonic-contrapuntal problem . . . a problem that may not admit of an elegant solution. But his attempt is worth a hundred would-be modern pieces that never show the slightest awareness of this problem's existence.'

Though I wrote that Inventions 2 and 4 are primarily harmonic, they present chordally accompanied melody which is symmetrically inverted: both melody and chords being inverted with total strictness. This technique was first codified by the German/American contrapuntist Bernhard Ziehn in *Canonic Studies* (Kaun, Milwaukee, 1912; second edition edited and introduced by Ronald Stevenson, Kahn & Averill, London, 1976). Ziehn's symmetrical inversion is the classical *contrarium reversum* chromatically expanded. Schoenberg's *Harmonielehre* borrows from Ziehn. Keller, a well-known Schoenbergian, doesn't mention Ziehn in the quoted review. Few 20th century composers have applied Ziehn's techniques: they include Bartók, Busoni – and Stevens.

The *Five Inventions* were sanctioned by the composer for performance on either piano or harpsichord. Harpsichordists looking for a ten-minute work in a still rather small 20th century repertoire might care to investigate it.

Ballad No 1 op 17 (1951)
Ballad No 2 op 42 (1969)

The composer, in a programme note, wrote that both these works were linked with the form of the Scottish folk-ballad: a series of 'verses' with a 'refrain' that gathers tension with repetition.

Op 17 begins with a four-bar 'refrain', setting a melody in stark octaves against an antiphonal chordal accompaniment. The harmonic progressions explore the relationship between two chords which have a common third, as in D minor to D flat major, or G major to G sharp minor. This 'refrain' functions as introduction, rondo theme and coda, always varied. After its initial appearance, a second subject is stated: a long, lyrical line which is evidence of Stevens' melodic gift. This expands the introduction's $^5/_4$ metre into $^2/_2$ $^3/_2$. It also expands the harmonic progression: the treble melody coils round the chords of E flat major to E minor (with a common third), underpinned by a tenor counter-melody and bass

arpeggiated accompaniment, which together trace the progression
B flat minor to A major (again with a common third: D flat and
C sharp).

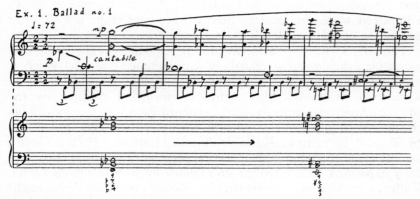

Ex. 1. Ballad no. 1

This is both bitonal *and* tonal. We have, together with the above
analysis, a second inversion of B flat minor with the major ninth
and major seventh above its bass, followed by a second inversion
of A major with the major ninth, major sixth and perfect fifth above
its bass. This has much more subtlety than mere bitonality.

After this long, periodic melody a development section follows
in quicker tempo, presenting invertible counterpoint mainly in
two voices, varied by monodic figuration and octave passages in
irregular metres and wide-ranging modulations. The recapitulation
of the 'refrain' in slower tempo is cast in neo-baroque double-dotted
bass octaves, underpinning clangorous chords of fourths and
sevenths. The second subject is recapitulated with melody and bass
in canon, with a reiterated inner chordal accompaniment between
the two outer parts. The 'refrain' makes its epilogic appearance in
the original *tempo adagio*, now moving from B flat minor to end in
G flat major: a case of Nielsenesque 'progressive tonality', for the
piece began on a chord of D minor. This piece is really a sonata
movement. It plays for twelve minutes, and is therefore only three
minutes shorter than Stevens' Piano Sonata.

Ballad No 2 is a shorter work, lasting seven minutes.

Examining Stevens' manuscripts, I found that the first page of
this piece utilised sketches from the composer's Cambridge years
in the Thirties. More than thirty years later he re-worked this
material. The form of Ballad No 2 is much the same as No 1, but

more concentrated. The opening eight-bar 'refrain' is chorale-like, with melody and bass in contrary motion. A two-bar phrase occurs in a succession of four keys, each a minor third higher than its preceding one: F – A flat – B – D. It is contrasted by *allegro* sections which occur between the 'refrain's' opening, three later statements, and a closing one. The first *allegro* is motoric with an ostinato staccato octave bass, and ejaculated, signal-like motifs in the right hand in tenor registers. The bass movement covers a minor third. The mainly two-part writing also explores bitonality of keys a third apart, e.g. C minor and E major. The enigmatic tritone also features. After the second 'refrain', now with treble and bass inverted, there follows a lyrical section with a melody in dotted rhythm and scalic progression, moving again through keys a third apart, e.g. E major to G minor. This reaches a climax which subsides with the third appearance of the 'refrain'; the lyrical section is recalled, varied and developed, reaching the main climax in big dramatic chords with 'Scots snap' rhythm, moving from E flat to F sharp and from D to F (again the all-pervasive third). The fourth 'refrain' is followed by a *presto* version of the opening *ostinato* passage which quickly achieves another climax, to plunge into the final refrain and brief coda in major/minor arpeggi, concluding on an open fifth chord on E, the tonal centre of the first *allegro*. The re-thinking of tonality in this work presents the opposition of the unambiguous keys of the 'refrain' and the ambiguous tonalities of the intervening sections.

Sonata in one movement op 25 (1954)

This might justifiably be called (in Medtnerian manner) a Ballad-Sonata. Like the two Ballads, it too has a 'refrain', a species of chorale in eight-part harmony, which 'pillars' the work in opening, central and closing appearances. The opening statement is cast in blocks of minor chords, on minor chords underpinned by augmented or diminished trials in middle or high register, thrice transposed in successive rhythmic diminution:

Ex. 2. Sonata

$3/2$ in minims, $4/4$ in crochets, $2/4$ in quavers; this rapidly builds up excitement, clinched by a bravura octave cascade that plunges into the first verse. This is a flowing texture of triplet scalic quavers, underpinning syncopated chords whose outline traces major or minor sevenths. Referring this flowing movement back to the opening chords, we discover it is made out of them entirely. It is as though, by analogy, the ice blocks of the opening chords were melted into flowing streams. Here I am forcefully reminded of some words of Carl Nielsen in his opuscule *Living Music* (translated from the Danish by Reginald Spink, Hutchinson, London, 1953, page 48): '. . . I have no doubt that the laws of the motions of the sea and air are reflected in every piece of good music of any length and symphonic extent.' The symphonic current of Stevens' Sonata is increased when the triplet quavers lead to semiquaver figuration, when thematic fragments are tossed about in the note-swirl, and when a bass ostinato breaks free of its repetition while maintaining its momentum.

Impetus gathers at the central 'refrain', even though it is slightly slower in tempo than the preceding verse. This impetus is achieved by omitting the 'refrain's' first bar and beginning at its second. The central *adagio* follows in contrasting linear writing. It sounds like new material, but underneath it is the same kind of chordal progression – movement by chords a third apart – that characterised the 'refrain'. This adagio is wrought in varied ternary form: its first section contrapuntal (over a palindromic ground bass – very rare), in three-part writing, mostly in low or middle register; its central section in treble and bass antiphony, with a syncopated chordal accompaniment in the middle of the texture; and the reprise to contrapuntal lines is at first in two, then three, essential voices, with octave doublings. A coda to the *adagio* reminisces on its central section, now in an organistic texture with big eight-part chords punctuating a melodic bass given in '4 foot', '8 foot' and '16 foot' octaves, all written on three staves. The variety of textures in this *adagio* is a master-lesson.

A transition leads to the final section, a $9/8$ jig of the Northumbrian sword-dance type, in C major with a characteristic Lydian fourth, F sharp, deriving from the tritone in the bass of the refrain. The jig's syncopations, though, are such as no sword-dance ever knew! A coda in slower tempo recalls the first 'verse'. Then the 'refrain's' first statement reaches the piano's highest register, now transposed from the opening E flat minor to A major (again the tritone relationship).

Nine Children's Pieces (1952)

One of Stevens' publishers, Lengnick, invited a group of their composers to contribute to a series of children's piano pieces, published as *Five Albums by Ten Composers*. Stevens furnished three easy pieces: *Round-About, Pipe & Drum* and *Haymakers' Dance*; three moderately easy pieces: *The Mirror* (canon), *Square Dance* and *Syncopation*; and three moderately difficult pieces: *Song without Words* and *Two Nocturnes*. His fellow-composers included such well-known figures as Alwyn, Arnold, Maconchy, Reizenstein, Rubbra and Wordsworth, and some lesser-known names. In contrast to the fanciful titles of some of his colleagues' pieces for children, Stevens had a 'no-nonsense' approach, addressed to such technical problems for tyro-pianists as equalisation of the hands. The means of achieving this end were Stevens' favoured devices of invertible counterpoint and canon by inversion.

Aria (c. early or mid 1960s)

The manuscript, like all of Stevens', is undated though a pencil manuscript of 1957 uses the same material, but without reference to a cryptogram which appeared later. The only clue to its finalisation date is a press cutting from the *Thames Gazette* (31 May 1966) reviewing a recital by the *Aria*'s dedicatee, Freda Swain, given by the Oxon and Bucks branch of the NEMO Music Society to mark its 100th concert in London and the provinces since its foundation in 1955. Freda Swain, its founder, played a group of pieces by Adrian Cruft, Gordon Jacob, Ian Parrott, Bernard Stevens and Guy Warrack, and Arthur Alexander played his own contribution. All the pieces were based on a cryptogram of four notes representing the name NEMO. In Stevens' piece it is traced in the bass in a falling third, G to E, and a rising third, F to A. The *Aria* is in ternary song form. Its flanking sections are in nocturne style, with a flowing treble melody in G with a C sharp Lydian fourth, accompanied by wide-spanning arpeggi. The central section is in G minor, and treats the bass motto-theme in chorale chords over a scalic bass in octaves. The reprise is varied, the Lydian inflection of the opening now becoming extended into a modulation from G to D flat; and there is a brief coda, referring to the chorale-like middle section.

This *Aria* would sound equally well – perhaps even better – on the concert harp. Harpists looking for an attractive three-minute piece to extend their somewhat limited repertoire of 20th century music might care to investigate this work.

Nocturne on a note-row of Ronald Stevenson op 51 (1979)

Stevens was interested in a song setting of mine to a poem by Hugh MacDiarmid. This was based on a twelve-note series containing all four kinds of triads: the augmented triad on F, E flat minor, the diminished triad on G sharp, and C major. My song presented these triads in close position. In his *Nocturne* Stevens extended them to open position for his widely-spaced arpeggio accompaniment. He presented the note-row in its clearest form at the centre of the *Nocturne* as a distillation. The piece is in varied ternary form with a quick middle section flanked by two slow ones. This *Nocturne* gives ample proof of Stevens' originality. He took material by another composer and transmuted it into something of his own. The reconciliation of dodecaphony with tonality is impressive.

Fuga alla Sarabanda (1980)
Elegiac Fugue on the name Geraldine (1981)

In the *Saraband-Fugue* Stevens re-addressed himself to the problem of squaring dodecaphony with tonality – a problem few composers have tackled (admittedly almost as impossible as squaring the circle!) The composer's manuscript bears the legend *soggetto dodecafonico*. The subject is in E minor/major. There are three 'voices'. The answer is given a tone higher. The subject's third appearance is given in the bass in D minor/major. As the theme is dodecaphonic, tonic/dominant hegemony is irrelevant. There is a counter-subject, though its recurrences are not strict as to pitch: it retains its identity by preserving its general outline and its syncopations. The exposition numbers eleven bars. The middle section has sixteen bars, as has the final section. The middle section modulates through the tonal centres of F sharp, A flat and F, with a significant augmentation of the *dux* in the bass in A flat minor/major, answered by a rhythmically varied *comes* in stretto. The subject is recapitulated in the bass with the answer in the treble, augmented in D flat minor/major. Towards the end there is a two-bar tonic pedal. The close is a simple perfect cadence in E major. With the final bass statement of the subject taken an octave higher than written, the whole fugue would be playable and effective on the harpsichord. A harpsichordist of enquiring mind could programme it with the Five Inventions.

The *Elegiac Fugue* on the name Geraldine was written and dedicated to the memory of Geraldine Peppin shortly after her death at the end of 1980. It could also be played on the organ or harpsichord, if it had 16-foot registration. This is a very lyrical fugue on a pentatonic subject. There are few accidentals throughout the piece, which gives it a strong modal flavour. The answer is given not in the dominant, but in the *sub*-dominant. There are four 'voices'. It is an extended fugue, 86 bars long. The exposition numbers 24 bars; the middle section 52 bars, and the final section 10 bars, with a *meno mosso* compensating for the foreshortening. The development section is really symphonic in 'feel', with big stretti over pedal-points. The final section, over a reiterated pedal-point, is grandly organistic. Indeed, this fugue is equally suitable to piano, concert harpsichord or organ.

A revised version of the *Elegiac Fugue* incorporated a quotation from Couperin's great *Passacaille* which sounds inevitable in context. It was a tribute to the Fugue's dedicatee, Geraldine Peppin, who frequently played this work;★ but it is also eloquent of Stevens' stature, that he can quote such a masterpiece without incongruity.

Fantasia on 'Giles Farnaby's Dreame', op 22 (1953)

Consideration of this Fantasia is placed out of chronology for three reasons:

> it relates to the *Elegiac Fugue* in so far as it quotes from early music;
>
> Stevens re-addressed himself to the Farnaby Fantasia

★ Shortly after playing the Elegiac Fugue at Geraldine's memorial meeting Bernard was playing the Couperin Passacaille in his studio, when by sudden insight, he realised that this theme combined perfectly with the theme derived from Geraldine's name. He came from the studio to tell me of this with considerable excitement, and that he had added a Coda combining the two themes. B.S.

in making a later version of it for chamber orchestra, re-titled *Introduction, Variations & Fugue on a theme of Giles Farnaby*, op 47 (1972);

and the work relates to the *Fantasia* for organ.

The first and last lines of the 24-bar melody of *Farnaby's Dreame* are:

Ex. 3. Fantasia, op. 22

The brief *adagio* introduction begins with the last line of the theme, transposed to C minor:

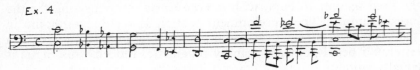

Ex. 4

This bears a relationship to the opening of Liszt's Piano Sonata in B minor:

Ex. 5

Farnaby's theme is given in its original harmony with octave doublings. There are eight variations.

Variation 1, *allegro*, is made out of the bass of the theme, treated in *ostinato*. Variation 2 is a carillon-chorale: the right hand having a carillon *ostinato* based on the theme's first line in variable accentuation; and the left hand having a chorale that sounds like a new theme but which, in fact, is a retrograde of the theme (compare with line 1 of ex.3):

Ex. 6
Allegro

Variation 3 has the character of a *perpetuum mobile*. Variation 4 is a 2-part invention with canonic entries at variable pitches. Variation 5 is a *scherzino* in 4-part writing, mainly in treble register and in changing metres. The tempo, which has so far been quick, slows down slightly in Variation 6, a *siciliano* with a canon repeatedly bandied from bass to treble. The slower tempo leads to Variation 7, which is a nocturne in G sharp minor – the furthest tonal remove from the theme's tonality of D major. Its texture – melody and bass lines with an internal, undulating *ostinato* – is very like that in the first song, *Comet Silence* (also a nocturne) of Stevens' song cycle *The True Dark,* op 49 (1974):

Ex. 7. Fantasia, op. 22
Adagio

"Comet Silence"

Variation 8 is a quasi-improvisation, an intermezzo, a moment of quietus. In *one* variation it is a *series* of variations on cadences:

Ex. 8 The right hand doubles at the octave higher
Adagio

This is almost oriental. To savour the harmonic originality, try playing (or getting somebody to play) that quotation in *E major*; then hear it as written and note the completely new sound achieved by the occasional use of a lowered semitone. This is mastery. So simple. So new.

A big crescendo leads to a brief cadenza in octaves – the one flash of virtuosity in the whole piece. This is broken off and a reminiscence of the introduction ushers in the extended fugal coda in D flat major, an expanded recapitulation of the theme with ornamentation in homage to the virginals composers of the sixteenth century.

This is an acid test: for a composer to base a work on a theme by a master of the past. Mediocrity will be outshone. New mastery will take its place beside a peer. Few 20th century composers survive this test. Few submit themselves to it. Stevens emerges undiminished. That is testimony to his stature.

Fantasia for organ, op 39 (1966)

Though not coming strictly within the purview of piano music, Stevens' only organ work is considered here, as its title connects it to the Farnaby Fantasia.

It belongs to the type of baroque *ricercar*, a compositional 'research' into contrapuntal skill. Like the mid-16th century *ricercar*, Stevens' is the instrumental equivalent of the vocal motet: indeed, the slower passages in this opus would work equally well if a text were set to them. They reveal the human voice behind Stevens' music. Like the *ricercari* in Bach's *Musical Offering* (1747), Stevens' work sometimes employs the 'vocal' notation of antique note-values (breves – seldom encountered in instrumental music).

The work's opening shows immediately how Stevens has the natural contrapuntist's craft of making multiple voices out of one line (here dodecaphonic *and* tonal),

which is essentially

Bach employed the same procedure in the Prelude in F, no 11 of Book 2 of the '48':

which is essentially

Stevens' short *adagio* introduction ushers in a chorale-prelude type of *allegro* presenting dance-like figuration over a pedal chorale. An *andante* 3-part invention follows. A reminiscence of the introduction leads to a 4-part fugue. Here the conjunct melodic motion of the introduction

is stretched into disjunct motion of 7ths:

The fugal subject and answer depart from the tonic-dominant ratio, as they do in Hindemith's *Ludus tonalis* (1942) for piano; e.g. the first answer is given a major 6th higher than the subject. A *poco più mosso* is cast in another 3-part invention which leads to a 3-part *pastorale* in $^{12}/_8$, beginning in A flat but with its tonality in constant flux. This flow subsides into a 4-part ostinato, quickening into a *più mosso* in $^2/_2$, a bridge passage employing homophony for the first

time in the work, and so building the climax, which is broken off
by a pedal cadenza of extensive melodic range. A quick section –
a third 3-part invention – introduces semiquavers for the first time
in the piece and is both *stretto* and *stretta*. Another cadenza (though
not so designated), this time for manuals, leads to a broad coda in
G sharp minor, with a *Tierce de Picardie* close. So the work is an
example of Nielsenesque progressive tonality, as it began on the
tonal centre of F.

In its 12 minutes the *Fantasia* has 12 sections, yet is almost
entirely monothematic: a master-lesson for any young composer.
It is perhaps the only 20th century organ work that can bear
comparison with Carl Nielsen's much longer *Commotio* (1931).

Canto di Compleanno (1974 transcription for piano solo by
Ronald Stevenson of *Birthday Song* for piano duet (1963); the title
translated into Italian to differentiate between the two versions).

This transcription was made in close consultation with, and was
approved by, the composer. He felt the opening accompaniment
figure

was in homage to Fauré. I feel the main melody

has a directness of appeal and a plasticity of contour such as could
ensure it the kind of success that Villa-Lobos' *Bachianas Brasileiras
No 5* has enjoyed, if only it were given the opportunity. The
association of the names Fauré and Villa-Lobos is not as curious as
it may seem: like Stevens, they both admired Bach; Villa-Lobos'
admiration is implicit in the title quoted, and Fauré (with Joseph
Bonnet) published an edition of Bach's organ works. The Stevens
Birthday Song is dedicated to Mary and Geraldine Peppin, whose
first names are contained in the main theme's cryptogram. The
transcriber dedicated his piano solo version to the composer's wife,
Bertha Stevens.

In the above guide to Stevens' solo piano works, I have tried to be objective. Such was my affection and admiration for both friend and musician, that I knew I had to keep firm hold on the reins of emotion, which, to be understood, needs face-to-face conversation: a voice rather than a pen; a glance, rather than cold print. I was fairly often Bernard's house-guest for two or three days at a time. We drank together at his 'local'. We walked the country lanes of Essex. We had some mighty fine exchanges of ideas. I miss them. I miss his unique blend of amiability and humour. He was an amusing raconteur and mimic. Only a modicum of his humour ever got into his music.

I'd like to share with you some of those exchanges of ideas we had, as background to my comments on his music.

Generally they took place in Bernard's music studio, a brick outhouse with a halfdoor. It was converted from a blacksmith's workshop. On a wall in the studio hung an old sepia photo of the actual blacksmith at work. The whole property is still called 'The Forge'. All this struck me as a happy coincidence, for Bernard, too, was a highly-skilled craftsman as a composer; something of a latter-day 'harmonious blacksmith'.

Unlike most musicians, he was deeply and widely read in English and American (and latterly in Oriental) literatures. [At Cambridge he had graduated in both Music and English.] He was the only musician who ever discussed with me Ezra Pound's opuscule *The Treatise on Harmony* (Covici, Chicago, 1927; Peter Owen, London, 1962). Some other musicians might have known that Pound was a major American poet of our age, but Bernard also knew that Pound had composed an opera (*Villon* – the music as well as the libretto) and had written this book on harmony. I recall Bernard's emphatic endorsement of Pound's postulation that

> A sound of any pitch, or any combination of such sounds, may be followed by a sound of any other pitch, or any combination of such sounds, providing the time-interval between them is properly gauged.

This rarely-mentioned ratio between harmony and the time-factor (or harmonic rhythm) lay behind another of our conversations, this time about the ending of Mahler's *Song of the Earth*. I love it to tears. Bernard didn't. He hazarded the conjecture that Mahler composed this (for Bernard) sickeningly prolonged peroration on the word *ewig* (eternally) out of his oft-repeated experience of conducting slow final curtains in the Vienna Opera House. An original observation. This must have been a strongly-held conviction, because not one Stevens composition has a drawn-out ending. Indeed, such was his abhorrence of this, to him, 'heart-on-the-sleeve' gesture, that his codas often seem fore-shortened to me. Sometimes, as at the close of the 2nd Ballad, he writes a sudden *adagio* for the last two bars or so which sometimes makes me wonder whether he experienced difficulty through some psychological inhibition about finishing a piece. I can't remember who it was who said, 'The coda is the most difficult thing to compose'.

On two occasions I found Bernard most provocative in question-time after public lectures of mine. The first occasion was at the British Institute of Recorded Sound in London. His aggressive question threw me. (I can't remember what it was.) The second occasion was at Essex University. I was ready for him this time and gave as good as I got. Afterwards, with his disarming smile, he said, 'You know, I didn't believe a word of that question of mine! I just wanted to get a discussion going'. Which he did. In argument he liked his opponent to stand up to him.

If there had been a British composer of the stature and fire of the artist William Blake as immediate precursor to Bernard Stevens, I think Bernard would have stood in relation to him as Blake's student Samuel Palmer did to Blake. But there was no such composer. Elgar's imperial aspect was unsympathetic to Bernard. Delius' voluptuous chromaticism was alien to him. Vaughan Williams, though admired by Bernard, was somehow too plain for him and lacked the mastery of Bernard's life-long aspiration: a sovereign command of counterpoint. What I mean by instancing the paintings of Samuel Palmer is that, though he will never be a big, marketable name (thank goodness!) he will always be an artist with a following of discerning adherents who value uniqueness when they experience it. So it is with Bernard Stevens' music.

Bernard had a wonderful smile. I believe all true musicians will feel it radiating to them when they perform his music; and, in performing it, I like to think that *his* smile will become *theirs*.

A genuine smile, in our troubled times, is worth something.

10

Piano Concerto and works for piano-duet and two pianos
Michael Finnissy

I

Why would the composer of a substantial, half-hour long, symphonically conceived Piano Concerto, brimming with noble and grandiloquent musical ideas, quite intricately cross-referenced thematic material, and yet typical of his accustomed tautness – conciseness – of utterance, make alterations to the work (as his last large-scale undertaking) effectively cutting the piece by a third, entirely sacrificing a sustained opening tutti equal to any other music he wrote, and generally re-balance and reduce the rôle of the piano soloist to an almost concertante one? Because the work belonged to a period of creative immaturity? No. The first version of Bernard Stevens' Piano Concerto dates from 1955, twelve years after the composition of the Violin Concerto, three years after the Cello Concerto, ten years after the First Symphony. It is roughly contemporary with two of his most extended, and arguably most accomplished, solo piano works – the Sonata op.25 and the *Fantasia on Giles Farnaby's Dreame* op.22.

There is nothing in the earlier version to suggest that Stevens was at all ill-at-ease with the medium, and nothing in the sketches reveals a troubled gestation. The answer to the question, if it can be answered at all, lies rather in the vexed area of 'performance practicality'; not merely of whether or not the solo part was too hard or too arduous (although this does seem to have been a consideration when making the revision), but whether the piece could be programmed at all. In spite of interest in the work at the time of its composition, it was not played, and neither version has received a public performance, although a studio recording of the revised version was made a few years ago by James Gibb and the BBC Welsh Symphony Orchestra conducted by Brian Wright.

In altering the piece, twenty-six years after writing the first version, Stevens did not re-fashion the musical ideas, and although a substantial amount of the solo part was removed, the orchestral writing was not modified. The major structural change consisted of deleting a large part of the opening, and replacing it with the original middle movement; instead of being divided into three movements the revised version is in two. The re-location of the central movement considerably alters the relationship between musical ideas presented as part of the original opening and re-stated in the final part of the work: the first span of an arch-like structure now being placed (and then *partially*, because shorn of its 'introduction') in the middle, while the middle has been moved forward to the beginning:

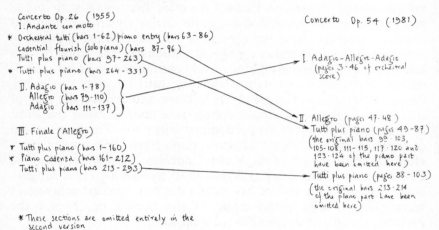

Concerto Op. 26 (1955)
I. Andante con moto
★ Orchestral tutti (bars 1-62) piano entry (bars 63-86)
cadential flourish (solo piano) (bars 87-96)
Tutti plus piano (bars 97-263)
★ Tutti plus piano (bars 264-331)

II. Adagio (bars 1-78)
Allegro (bars 79-110)
Adagio (bars 111-137)

III. Finale (Allegro)

★ Tutti plus piano (bars 1-160)
★ Piano Cadenza (bars 161-212)
Tutti plus piano (bars 213-293)

Concerto Op. 54 (1981)

I. Adagio-Allegro-Adagio
(pages 3-46 of orchestral score)

II. Allegro (pages 47-48)
Tutti plus piano (pages 49-87)
(the original bars 99-103, 105-108, 111-115, 117-120 and 123-124 of the piano part have been omitted here)
Tutti plus piano (pages 88-103)
(the original bars 213-214 of the piano part have been omitted here)

★ These sections are omitted entirely in the second version

The style of the piano writing is designed to match the orchestra on an equal footing; it is grand, heroic, muscular and weighty, requiring strength and intensity rather than flash-and-filigree finger technique. In this it seems most obviously descended from the two Brahms concerti – the virtuosity rarely being overtly 'on display'. I recall Stevens' interest in, and enthusiasm for the second Brahms concerto in particular – with its close-knit, almost at times chamber-music-like integration of piano and orchestra, its seriousness of dialectic, and its purely musical – rather than its less obvious quasi-dramatic – skill. What has been omitted in the second version that particularly involves the soloist? At the 63rd bar the piano enters with an upward-scale flourish, and from bars 65 to 86 carries the main melodic weight of the music over a lightly scored accompaniment. Bars 264 to 331 recall the music of bars 97 to 263 – the piano again playing constantly and carrying much of the main melodic weight. The quasi-arpeggio figuration of bars 97 and 98 is, in the first version, repeated – with changing harmonies – throughout bars 99 to 125. After six bars of orchestral introduction the piano also carries the main melodic ideas in the opening of the Finale, with two brief respites between bars 61 and 75, and bars 121 and 160. The cadenza is ruminative, preparing the way for the eventual juxtaposition of material from first and last movements that Stevens effects with the re-entry of the orchestra.

The predominant colours of the Stevens Piano Concerto are sombre and meditative, dark rather than bright; although I have mentioned Brahms as a possible influence, the concerti of Busoni and, closer to home, Tippett are not dissimilar in character.

From the cut-up score of the first version that goes to make the second I would guess that the revision was a rather perfunctory affair. It would not seem that Stevens agonised greatly over re-modelling the work afresh, but took an expedient – albeit rather drastic – solution to try and get the work performed. Having studied both versions I can find no reason to prefer the second, nor consider it an improvement on the original 1955 score. The best advocate for the original version is, of course, the music itself. It is impossible to quote all the fine stuff that Stevens cut from the revised version, but surely to lose this, the abandoned opening of the work, would be lamentable:

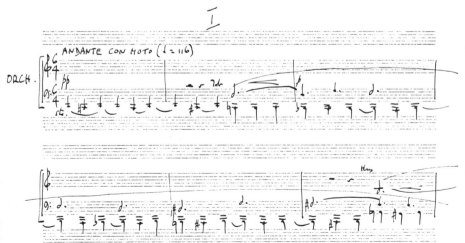

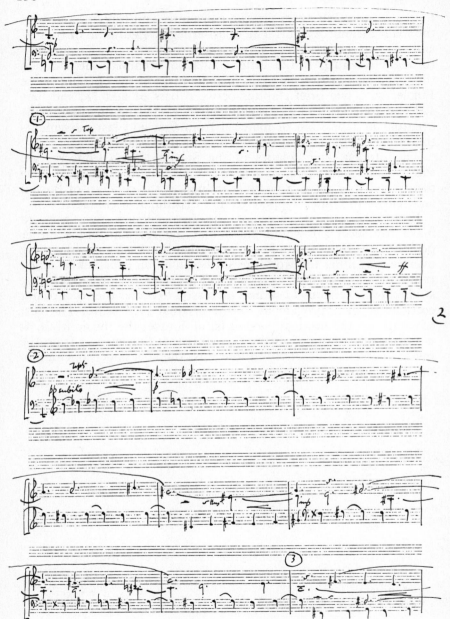

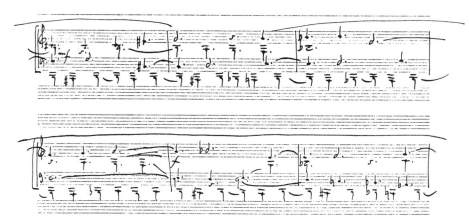

II

Piano duet – four hands at one piano – is still a medium more likely to suggest the drawing-room and amateur music-making – perhaps, too, those unjustly sneered at piano reductions of symphonies, quartets and overtures – rather than professional and 'serious' concert-giving. Indeed there are a number of manuscript arrangements of orchestral works (both his own and, amongst others, by Rubbra) by Stevens – though I propose here to discuss only those works originally conceived for piano duet, at least one of which I consider worthy to stand alongside the Sonatas and Variations by Mozart and Schubert that form such a similarly neglected part of their output through being cast in this genre.

Both of the extended pieces for two pianos are major statements, the *Introduction and Allegro* being eventually re-cast as *Choriamb* op.41 for orchestra – prompting the question of why this period of composition 1955-57 (opp.26-29) should be so disturbed by later adaptations and revisions?

The piano writing in both sets of pieces is beautifully conceived for the instrument, and well structured to give both players equal weight and responsibility. Stevens seems to prefer the piano's darker hues – as Alkan and Busoni also do – but the colouring is never monotone, and the pieces enjoy a degree of brilliance and virtuosity which is a natural, exuberant outgrowth of the music's forward momentum – never merely splashy or to be confused with outbursts of bad temper.

Fantasia on the Irish Ho-Hoane op.13 for piano-duet (1949)

The Irish Ho-Hoane was in all probability a folk-tune, but in its
present incarnation it is to be found as the 26th piece in Volume
1 of the Fitzwilliam Virginal Book, though in G minor; Stevens
transposes it to A flat minor and omits the embellishments, credited
to 'Anon.'.

I think that this Fantasia, commissioned by Paul Hamburger
and Helen Pyke, is one of Stevens' finest achievements. It was the
first of a number of pieces he wrote between 1949 and 1953 based
on 16th and early 17th century themes. It is certainly one in which
fluent invention, contrapuntal mastery, vitality and interest are not
foreshortened by formal concision and emotional intensity.

After an Introduction and the statement of the theme itself,
there are seven continuous 'variations' – seven responses to the
anonymous (dance?) tune. The Introduction (*Andante, con molto
rubato ed espressione*) seems to be quietly searching for the melody:
its quintuple measure, the initial beat of each bar embellished with
a mordent, and its gently meandering unharmonised line, create
a feeling of hesitant expectancy, resolved by the entry of the
Ho-Hoane at the seventh bar. The first variation is quite intricate,
making quirky textural use of staccato semiquavers (located first in
the twenty-first bar of the original material's bass-line) as intrusions
in an otherwise *sempre legato* flow of imitative counterpoint,
underpinned with open fifths:

The second, very brief, variation is canonic and very wittily
contrived. The third variation is much more extended, with
slower melodic derivations of the original theme floating across
shifting, rapid, ostinato-like patterns – grouped in four quavers
(♪♪♪♪ ♪♪♪♪). The fourth variation, again quite brief, introduces
odd bars of ⅝ and ⁶/₈ into an otherwise constant ⁴/₈ ♫ ♫ pulse
that continues, without a break, from the previous variation,
the material (staccato chords) exchanged between the players
in dialogue. The fifth variation, also fairly short and compact,
elaborates on the irregular pulsing of variation four: its metre constantly shifting ⁷/₈ ⁴/₈ ⁵/₈ ⁷/₈ ⁴/₈ - - - ³/₄ ⁴/₈ ⁴/₈ ³/₄ ⁴/₄ ⁴/₄. The sixth variation
(*Adagio*) is more extended. Against a constant ³/₄ ♫♫♫♫♫ pulsing
in the upper bass register, two sustained lines – one high, one low
– move, at one bar's distance, in canon – the top line being an
(occasionally rather free) inversion of the bottom one. The final
variation (*Allegro*) reverts to denser four-part polyphony, resolutely

progressing towards the majestic closing bars, where the *Allargando* should perhaps start to be felt, and be played thus, two or three bars earlier than marked, in order not to seem too peremptory.

Two Dances op.33 for piano-duet (1962)

These are dances more of the elements – 'cosmic' dances – than of human dancers or dances of the ballroom. Stevens seemed interested in a very fundamental, organic, relationship of dance to music, as located in tribal ritual or folk ceremony, or even more simply expressed in the release of impulsive energy in almost *any* human or animal or elemental movement. Certainly the underlying structure of these short pieces (3½ and 2 minutes respectively) is primarily rhythmic – although this does not mean that the sound-fabric avoids intricate, even occasionally quite convoluted, polyphonic textures.

The first dance is an *Andante con moto* in triple metre, the melodic material often shared, in canon, between the two players. It has considerable charm in its lilting melancholy, the rather short-breathed phrases, enigmatic rather chromatic harmonies, rising tritones and falling ninths – very generally reminding me of late-period Rachmaninoff, perhaps appropriately enough the *Symphonic Dances* in particular.

If I was, perhaps inappropriately, reminded of Rachmaninoff by the first dance, how much more inappropriate is my reaction to the second, an *Allegro* in irregular metres – which sounds, to me, a lot like one of Conlon Nancarrow's rhythm-studies for player-piano? As a teacher Bernard Stevens had one of the most wonderfully and fascinatingly filled and eclectic minds I've ever encountered, and he could never be found wanting in response to even the most esoteric, generally unheard-of, merely eccentric, or ideologically way-ahead-of-its-time notions: so it is more than likely that he knew about Nancarrow's music, a long time before it became an underground cult or was widely enough broadcast to be considered popular. Such irrelevant speculation aside, the pre-occupation of both Stevens and Nancarrow with intricate contrapuntal 'mechanisms', especially canon, is very similar. In a programme note Stevens wrote that these dances were composed as studies in rhythmical application of the ideas of bodily movement of Rudolf Laban, the Czech choreographer. He also developed these ideas in his *Dance Suite* for orchestra and Second Symphony.

Birthday Song for piano-duet (1963)

Mary and Geraldine Peppin, for whom this was written, had given
the first performance of the *Introduction and Allegro* for two pianos,
and it was Geraldine's death that prompted the *Elegiac Fugue* for
solo piano (1981). The main material is a theme containing the
names MARY-GERALDINE as derived from a white-note musical
alphabet:

The piece is simpler in texture, and more uniformly lyrical
in expression – songlike as the title suggests – than the other
works under discussion here. Each of the two main sections
begins with a statement of the MARY-GERALDINE theme over a
rocking accompaniment – Schubertian in its easy-going simplicity.
A rising theme, first heard in bar 10 of the Primo part, then starts
off a more intense chordal episode, leading to a *fortissimo* climax,
which quickly subsides into the second main section (starting at bar
28). This pattern is repeated, though not with identical material,
subsiding after a second climax into a third statement of the theme
(at bar 55), this time with E flats rather than E naturals, the theme
rising and transforming itself into a serene valedictory coda, 3 bars
in length, ending in F major.

Introduction and Allegro op.29 for two pianos (1957)

Stevens' own succinct comments on this work refer to the interplay between $^3/_2$ $^6/_4$ and $^{12}/_8$ metres – characteristic, however, of most of his music in triple-time, and perhaps reflecting his great interest in the music of the Elizabethan period, late sixteenth and early seventeenth century rhythmic devices (stresses and syncopations) in general, or indeed even earlier metrical intricacies and cross-rhythms in the music of John Dunstable or the Flemish school.

The piece begins (*Adagio*) very characteristically with a slowish melody unfolding in alternations of fourths and semitones, which then provide motivic material for further counterpoints and counter-subjects:

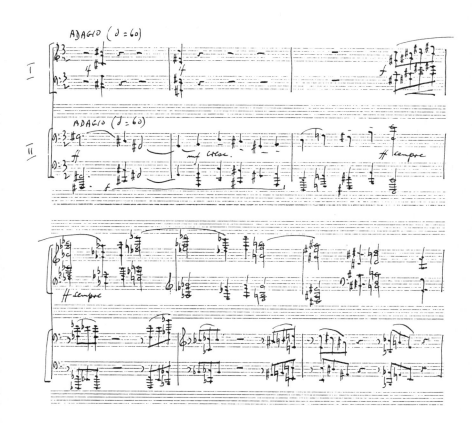

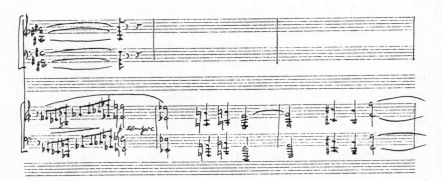

This stately introduction, lasting 26 bars, seems to be entirely fashioned from the initial material, the very opening of which appears again (though more than twice as fast) as the initial theme of the *Allegro deciso*, accompanied by a much busier, denser, polyphony. The contrasting central Legato episode of this main *Allegro* is, in fact, at a faster tempo (♩ = 240 compared with ♩ = 144 of the *Allegro deciso*) although the welter of activity subsides to a sufficient degree for it, in effect, to seem slower. Its music, too, stems from the reservoir of material generated by the opening – fourths and semitones, with a particular emphasis here on a repeated rising semitone. The return of the *Allegro deciso* is seamlessly effected, component fragments of the initial melody being endlessly varied and recombined. The rising semitone of the central episode is much in evidence again in the *Più Mosso* Coda which brings the work to a close, not unusually with a diatonic resolution in the final rallentando.

Stevens later orchestrated this work, as *Choriamb* op.41, his later title revealing a little of the character of the piece: a kind of invocation of an ancient choral dance, perhaps a Dionysian ceremony, the frenzied conclusion of which is almost abrupt and surprisingly perfunctory. In the later, orchestral, version Stevens added about three minutes music – most of it to the *Allegro*, and seemingly designed to expand, and possibly clarify, the somewhat compressed, dense and highly charged harmonies of the original.

Concertante op.55 for two pianos (1982)

This three-movement piece was Stevens' last composition. It was written in Menorca in June 1982, although the final pencil-score lacked dynamic markings and phrasing, which he was too ill to add before he died in the following January, and which were eventually added by the dedicatees, Isabel Beyer and Harvey Dagul, and by Bertha Stevens.

As with *Birthday Song* and *Elegiac Fugue*, the main melodic material is based on the names of the dedicatees who commissioned it, on this occasion derived from a *chromatic* musical alphabet:

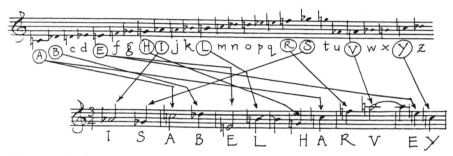

Stevens had experimented with the white-note alphabet that he had used in the earlier pieces in one of the first sketches for this piece, but the melodic shapes that resulted:

were either unsatisfactory, or uninspiring.

The first movement (*Andante con moto* 3/4) is a passacaglia on the six-bar ISABEL-HARVEY theme. The theme, first stated in bare octaves in the bass register, gradually yields a harmonic sequence – modulating away from F sharp (minor) firstly towards E (minor), then C (minor), then D (minor), and finally to a sort of dominant seventh on C at the cadence back to F sharp at the start of each subsequent variation. The tonalities are hinted at rather than explicit, the ever skilful contrapuntal play dominating the texture. At the tenth variation the metre changes to 12/8 (*sotto voce*) where a ground bass derived from a 'verticalisation' of the name-theme provides the main motivic material:

The eleventh and concluding twelfth variation return to the opening metre and tonality, ending affirmatively in F sharp major.

The central *Adagio* consists of a long wide-ranging melody, 38 bars in length, accompanied by a steady, even relentless, flow of 3-note minim chords. The melody itself is – effectively – unbroken, though made up of continuous variations of the component intervals of the inversion of the ISABEL-HARVEY theme.

The atmosphere of the music seems remote and distant – quite eschewing the contrapuntal excitements of the flanking movements, and intensely concentrated and rather disturbing in its unadorned, sculpted marble, simplicity.

The final *Presto* begins with a chain of dance-like (9/8) variations, in many respects like reminiscences of the opening Passacaglia and, in fact, derived from the mass of counter-subjects to the main theme of that movement, culminating in a cadenza-like episode:

after which the closing three variations (the first and third of which are in a slightly slower tempo and more clearly refer to the ISABEL-HARVEY theme) lead to a majestic coda on a pedal F sharp, very like the first conclusion of the *Elegiac Fugue*.

I have attempted, in the foregoing, a fairly objective and, because of restrictions of space, not too detailed or extended commentary on a specific area of Bernard Stevens' music. Even if, as a writer *of* music, I was not painfully aware of the limitations and difficulties of writing *about* music, I would nonetheless have found this task a difficult one. Bernard Stevens was my teacher, and I still hold him in awe and respect. I would not venture to know how to assess *critically* his position in the history of music – even the more limited history of twentieth century music, or just of that period *in England*; presumption of that kind I would, in any case, view with a jaundiced eye.

It is almost certainly true that now – 1988 – is too soon to view his music with sufficient perspective. To try and focus my own response to it I have – with some reservation, I'll admit – referred to a few other composers whose works have sounds and colours in common with his, or so it seems to me. The great technical strengths of his work – his counterpoint, his architectural concision – might, by overfed cynics, be considered dry or too intellectual. But it is the corollary of these qualities, it is the emotional intensity of Stevens' music – that fierce, dark melancholy, a characteristic of his soul-mate Dowland – that has emblazoned itself on my heart and memory, and it is that I most cherish and find my life most enhanced by when I listen to, or play it.

11
An Excursion into Film Music
Bertha Stevens

After Bernard's success with his first symphony, he was immediately asked to write the music for a feature film in which James Mason not only starred but had considerable influence on the production. Mason's work in that role was as meticulous as his acting in this, *The Upturned Glass* (1947). He was keenly interested and involved in the music. It was a gripping film, and the emotional span of the music had to range from spine-chilling suspense, complex psychological emotional disturbance, deep romantic passion, 'brain operation' music and a rumba as party background music to charming piano pieces for a child which transformed into wild emotional outbursts on the piano played by the hero (James Mason). Of course the composer had the fun of 'ghosting' the piano playing.

This was quite a challenge for a young composer writing for his very first film. There was another challenge. Early 1947 was cold, and there were power cuts in London because of fuel shortages – an aftermath of the war. This created difficulties as film music frequently has to be written over-night, ready for rapid copying and recording, following a day at the studios watching 'rushes'. Bernard once was phoned at night and asked for three piano pieces by the morning. For these overnight sessions there was frequently very little light – sometimes only candles, and screens round, making a little corner by a very small fire on which we brewed hot drinks. The conditions seemed centuries away from the work in hand.

But Bernard was fortunate in having good opportunities for discussion with Mason, who used to call for him in his car or taxi to go to the studios, and there was considerable sympathy between them. Needless to say, he could only treat this writing as a creative challenge, seeking to produce music of real artistic value. I am told on excellent authority that Mason considered this film one of his best, and that it did much to help establish him in the American film industry. He seems to have been well satisfied with the music, and wrote from America:

Sir Keith Falkner introducing Bernard to H.M. The Queen Mother.
The beautiful damask doctorate robes he is wearing were first worn by
Thomas Attwood Walmisley in 1848 and owned by Vaughan Williams.
(Copyright: the Royal College of Music)

We saw the completed *Upturned Glass* last night and hasten to report complete satisfaction with your music. It had great charm and freshness and honestly reflected the atmosphere throughout. It was a terrific job and I do hope that you'll do some more films. Or did the experience madden you?

Scott Goddard wrote in Penguine Music Magazine:

In the meantime, Bernard Steven's music for *The Upturned Glass* was showing what an intelligent manipulation of music could produce in the way of emphasis and suggestion. This was, in fact, the right way of bending music to the producer's will. Viewed as a whole the film had plenty of excellent silences. After the tepid wash of continual music in other films, the effect of the first of these silences was dazzling. One realised that the music was being treated seriously, utilised with care, dispensed with if all it could do at a given moment would be to become a meaningless chit-chat.

Following this, in the same year, Bernard was asked to write for *The Mark of Cain* starring Eric Portman. The amount of music required was considerable, including an imitation Tchaikovsky piano concerto demanded by the director, who would not have the real thing.

This was the period in feature films when dramatic highlights frequently took place at concerts, with the stars looking extremely glamorous in full evening dress, expressing suitable emotional reactions to the romantic music! Although it is encouraging that the leading characters in a film are shown as being appreciative of cultural activities in the form of attending orchestral concerts, in *The Mark of Cain* it was merely used as a means of displaying their personal glamour. This is in contrast to the much more meaningful use of music in *The Upturned Glass*, where the actual activity of the characters playing music was used as an integral part of the expression of their emotional conflict. Bernard produced a good concerto piece, and one regrets that, although pencil sketches of his film music exist, the scores along with hundreds of others automatically taken into possession of the film companies have been lost.

I recently had the privilege of seeing the films again at the National Film Archive. There was much good music in *The Mark of Cain*, well played by the LSO but wasted by an incompetent director. Apart from Portman's skill as an actor, the rest of the cast were surprisingly ineffective. I think it was while working on this film that Bernard's irritation was so great that as he left Denham railway station on the way to the studios after a night composing, he suddenly took his score from his case, tore it in half and threw it in a hedge. This film was not a happy episode in his life!

But of course money was very helpful to a young composer just out of the army, and so the next year he took on another film, *Once a Jolly Swagman* based on a novel by Montague Slater. This time he was working with a better team, but less music, in fact one could almost say too little, was demanded. Dirk Bogarde starred as a brash young dirt track rider, formerly a factory worker, being trained for stardom by a played-out Australian coach who had lost his nerve (Lag Gibbons). This part was wonderfully played by Bill Owen, who started his career in the little left-wing Unity Theatre at King's Cross before World War II. An arrangement of the Australian song *Waltzing Matilda* was required to track in with episodes relating to the rather poignant character of Lag, and this music proved profitable to Bernard for many years in Australia. Once again the director (Ian Dalrymple) was delighted with the ingenuity of the music.

But Bernard had had enough, and firmly refused to continue with film music. He felt there were few directors who used their composers well as they so frequently used music vulgarly to divert attention from the inadequacies of their films, and that much could be learned from the discreet use of music in French films. He preferred to accept a teaching post at the Royal College, where he took over pupils of his former professor R.O. Morris, to supplement what resulted from his true path of composition – and he was a born educator.

Regret for this decision has been expressed by those who have heard his film music, as they consider he wrote well for the medium.

12

The Shadow of the Glen: Opera in One Act
Christopher De Souza

'Opera is a wonderful medium. The finest expression of what human relationships are all about', said Bernard Stevens in a newspaper interview in January 1974 when he was working on his only complete stage work, *The Shadow of the Glen*. And nearly ten years before that, in another interview with a local Essex paper, his great interest in opera is mentioned, and his feeling that he might be stimulated to write one if a good libretto came his way. What this article did not say was that he had been looking for a good libretto for close on twenty years by then.

As a graduate from Cambridge in both English and Music, his concern to find fitting texts is understandable, but as other composers, notably Britten, had solved the problem many times over by 1965, there must surely be a deeper reason for his reticence.

The evidence of Stevens' search for an opera text goes back to as early as 1947. Through his cultural activities with the left-wing movement (he had joined the Communist Party in 1943, while serving in the Army) he had formed a close friendship with Montague Slater and, in 1945 to 1946, Jack Lindsay, a director of Fore Publications who produced such magazines as *Our Time* and *Arena*. Slater had been writing films for the Ministry of Information, and Lindsay had been a writer for the Army Bureau of Current Affairs.

'After the War', Bertha Stevens says, 'there was a great feeling of liberation and enthusiasm, a feeling that the brave new world could be built . . . commercial interests were at a low ebb, and not in control of people's lives, which gave a chance for imagination and creative enthusiasm. There seemed there could be a popular advance, a possibility of people themselves widely using their creative gifts and power'. At this time Stevens was writing and arranging the music for the pageants that Slater and Lindsay organised for the Left-wing movement at Haringay and Earls Court. The project that appears to have brought them together was

Examining young candidates in Maseru, Lesotho 1968.

born of their shared enthusiasm for the novel Lindsay published in 1938, covering the year of the 1649 rebellion, which they hoped would serve as the basis for a musical work, but other projects got in the way, and only a detailed typescript treatment remains among the composer's papers.

Lindsay, the artist Paul Hogarth, the poet Randall Swingler, the composer Alan Rawsthorne, and Stevens all ended up living near one another in Essex. There were intense philosophical and artistic discussions late into the night, and many ideas must then have been mooted as suitable bases for opera libretti. A letter from Lindsay survives among Stevens' papers which suggests they had already been discussing a project for an historical opera; Cromwell is the subject proposed in Lindsay's letter, and the treatment outlined is very similar to that it received from David Storey in his 1973 play 'Cromwell'. Lindsay also sent Stevens two interlinked libretti for two 'Nordik' pieces, one called *Hate*, the other *Love*, but nothing seems to have come of either. Intriguingly, among the composer's papers there is a translation by Montague Slater and David Magarshak of Pushkin's *Mozart and Salieri*. Stevens did at least begin an opera in 1950 as an entry in a competition organised by the Arts Council of Great Britain. He greatly admired Slater's libretto for Benjamin Britten's *Peter Grimes*, and so it was natural that he should involve him in this project.

The piece was to have been called *Mimosa*. Among the composer's papers are four foolscap folders. A grey-green one contains a cast-list, Slater's short story, a 'Synopsis of Dramatic Action and Musical Treatment', and a fourth section labelled 'Fragment of Act One'. All this has been professionally prepared in blue-black and red typescript. The cover reads 'Mimosa: an Opera in Three Acts. Libretto by Montague Slater. Music by Terpander.' Clearly this was a pseudonym* for the purpose of the competition and the material submitted to the jury. Another red folder contains a carbon copy of the story. A third, blue/grey, has carbon copies of the cast list and synopsis of treatment. A fourth pink folder contains a carbon copy of the 'Fragment of Act One'. There is also a complete foolscap libretto for Act Two.

The story concerns rum politicking in a small sub-tropical

---

* Terpander was a Greek poet and musician, regarded as the founder of Greek classical music and of lyric poetry. Stevens always used this pseudonym.

island around 1910. Mimosa seems to be an amalgam of Malta
and the West Indies, via somewhere like Fernando Po, where the
sophisticated cultural and political elite mix politics and love, at
the expense and in spite of the local peasantry. The hero is one
Paul Umana, a sort of political Everyman as his surname implies;
his person and the story are, in fact, clearly based on the career of
the Irish patriot, Charles Stewart Parnell, and the action, according
to the synopsis, 'takes place entirely in the Hotel Bristol (its cafe
and restaurant) in Mimosa, in the Square of the Duomo'.

The next paragraph of the 'Synopsis of Dramatic Action and
Music Treatment' is 'Verse Form'. The form used is four-beat
couplets in half-rhymes (the form devised for *Peter Grimes*). 'This
is the form of the recitatives and some of the numbers, though the
set numbers as a rule will have other metres.'

The libretto clearly was not finished at this stage, and as
nothing survives of the rest of Act One or of Act Three among
the composer's papers, it does not seem ever to have been finished.
What we have is only selected draft material for submission to the
competition jury, which, had it been successful, would then have
been completed.

It was not successful, and there is a letter from E.J. Dent
in Bertha Stevens' possession which explains it all. Dent had
been one of Stevens' tutors at Cambridge, and they had, of
course, discussed opera. In an interview Stevens said that Dent
expressed the opinion that there was most future for opera in the
development of chamber opera. Dent was on the jury for the Arts
Council competition, and I surmise that after his project had been
turned down, Stevens wrote to Dent to find out why. His reply is
of great interest, both as an example of Dent's critical stance and
acumen, and as a commentary on 20th century opera in general,
and some of its popular successes in particular.

17 Cromwell Place
London SW7
12 June 1950

Dear Bernard

I had no idea that you were the intending composer of *Mimosa*.
I can't tell you very much; I have really forgotten what the other
members of the Jury said about it, and if I could remember, I

[would] have to regard it as confidential. But I kept a copy of my own report and have looked at it again, and as the opera was rejected on the libretto alone, I don't think I am committing a breach of confidence in giving you my own impression of it. We never saw a note of the music, as far as I remember.

The libretto reminded me very much of the sort of operas that were being produced in Berlin about 1920-25, all trying desperately hard to be 'modern' in what I might call the 'Grand Hotel' style. (One was actually called *Grand Hotel*.) *Mimosa* seemed to be designed for very luscious imitation Puccini combined with cynical musical comedy.

The short story was rather like an attempt to imitate Somerset Maugham, but extremely complicated and elliptical in style – I found it very difficult to follow. If it was made into a play it would be still more difficult to understand, and if into an opera of course far worse.

The difficulty of the plot itself was further complicated by the perpetual intrusion of Slater himself with the expression of his own private philosophy – very interesting to read at leisure, but simply unintelligible and probably inaudible if sung. It seemed to me quite hopeless as a libretto [to] set to music. What made it worse was the frequent introduction of 'songs' of some sort for subsidiary characters, just introduced for the sake of a song that could be applauded and made into a gramophone record. There was also an absurd chorus of journalists and harlots in the manner of a Tuscan *stornello* – 'Flower of the something or other' – a verse form peculiar to Tuscany and in this situation just a secondhand literary affectation.

I have been reading fifty or sixty opera librettos and almost as many operas, and what always infuriates me is the obvious aiming at some already hackneyed popular effect of commercial opera. *Peter Grimes* held me (and I saw three different productions, two in London and one in Budapest, which was the best of all by far) by its sincerity and integrity as a whole, though I was annoyed by certain tricks of effect at times.

I come to the conclusion that it is a mistake to try to write highly 'poetical' and 'literary' librettos. The poet ought to concentrate entirely on drama and absolute truth to human nature, however unreal or fantastic the story may be; and always to use the very simplest words which everybody can understand at first hearing.

Secondly, always to make the characters talk in their own character, and to avoid carefully all temptation to put the author's own private philosophy of life into their mouths. This if properly carried out does not at all prevent the poet's own personality coming through the whole drama, as the great dramatists of the past have shown us. Prospero for instance talks a good deal of 'philosophy' but it is all within the character of Prospero himself.

One bad fault of *Peter Grimes*, I thought, was that the minor characters like Auntie and Boles so often talk *at* each other, and *to* the audience, and do not really engage in conversation, talking *to* each other. But perhaps Slater would reply that people of their education and manners do very often express their feelings regardless of the people they are talking with, and do just talk into the blue. But I can't think it makes good drama on the stage.

Much the same applied to the chorus at times, especially in the scene following the Inquest (and during the Inquest – though I must say the Inquest scene is masterly as a whole and about the best 'exposition' of an opera I have ever known) where they have a long sustained tune. It is a poor tune, and you don't really hear any words; it is really a survival (to some extent modernized) of the old-fashioned 'opening chorus' of soldiers, gipsies or 'gentlemen of Japan'. The other bad patch, I always felt, was the much admired ensemble of the women after the men go off to lynch Peter at the hut. I find it musically boring and vocally ill-contrived, also utterly static; and it is inappropriate that Ellen should join in block harmony with Auntie and the nieces. The Budapest producer at least had the sense to make her stand very much apart from them.

Boles was always a great character thrown away. When I went to the preliminary lecture at the Wigmore Hall, before the first S[adlers] W[ells] production, and extracts were sung, I got the impression that Boles (very well sung by Morgan Jones) was going to play a great part in the opera; but he didn't, and at C[ovent] G[arden] it was worse still, because the part was sung by....

Why has Britten dropped Slater as a librettist? If they had gone on working together we might have had another opera on the level of *Grimes* and better, if they both learned (and in collaboration) something from experience. But with Ronald Duncan poor B.B. fell out of the frying-pan into the fire, and every mistake of inexperience made by him with Slater was intensified instead of being corrected. I enjoyed *Herring* as an amusing triviality but don't think I want to see it again; *Lucretia* is just dreadful. I saw *Grimes* about a dozen times and was always deeply gripped and moved by it.

I can't think how *you* of all people came to be attracted by *Mimosa*, for such music of yours as I have heard has always had a certain severity and austerity of style which I very sincerely respected, even if critics said it was was dry and academic. I am glad you want to write opera; it may loosen your joints a bit, and at the same time we badly need integrity and sincerity in opera.

Fidelio is still the greatest of all. And there is certainly integrity in *Trovatore*, *Carmen*, *Aida*, *Eugene Onegin* and *Boris Godunov*. Also in *Wozzeck*, *Pelléas* and Bartók's *Bluebeard*.

Yours

Edward Dent

This letter must have been of cardinal importance to Stevens' development, and one can imagine that he would have subjected each subsequent operatic proposal to the closest critical scrutiny with his old professor's words very much in mind.

As I said, this letter explains it all; but there is a little mystery that is not quite explained. Eight letters exist recording the progress of his entry into the Arts Council commission. On 11 May 1949 Eric Walter White wrote to tell him his application was approved. On 20 June he wrote to remind him the closing date was 30 June, and on 1 July wrote a third time to ask whether the entry was on its way. It was, and a letter of 4 July acknowledges receipt. Two months later, on 15 September, White wrote again stating that the judges were 'interested in the libretto but feel they can make a satisfactory judgement only if they see something substantial in the way of music'. A follow-up on 22 September asks Stevens please to begin composition (he was very busy at the time), and to send what he could by 24 October. A letter from the Arts Council of that date acknowledges receipt of part of the piano score (evidently the pages we have noted already). Only ten days later, to judge from a letter of 11 November, this music had been seen and discussed, and dismissed by the judges – or had it? Dent seems to imply not, and that sentence in his letter of June 1950 must have seemed curious to Stevens after going to so much trouble to send some music in.

Surprisingly he does seem to have continued to work on *Mimosa* at least up to the end of 1951, eighteen months after receiving Dent's letter. He had been working on setting some of Slater's verse, and in a letter to Stevens of 19 December 1951 Slater adds a postscript asking whether he had any comments on Act 2, and for the return of what appeared to be the only remaining copy of it. As there is still a copy among Stevens' papers, it cannot have been returned, and for one reason or another work on *Mimosa* came to a halt. Possibly Stevens never mentioned Dent's letter to Slater, and Slater, unaware, went on with preparing Act 2 until other work simply displaced it. Dent's sagacity and wisdom is tantalisingly borne out by the pencilled sketches Stevens has left of two parts of Act 1: the necessity to think big does indeed seem to have loosened his joints. There are 56 bars of the opening of the opera and no fewer than 252 bars of a later section of Scene One. The music has a broad flow and fluency and there are hints in the sketches of an attractive instrumentation.

His collaboration with Slater achieved permanence in the song-cycle *The Palatine Coast* of 1952, the second song of which is directly related to *Mimosa*.

MIMOSA: Act I, Scene 1

Finally, mention must be made of the many other texts collected by the composer, ranging from Blake to Spender, which show his wide literary knowledge, and sympathies. What all the poems have in common is a palpable expression of the experience of love, from the deep physicality of Spender's *Daybreak*, through what Slater called his own 'vague fleshiness', to a broader comprehension of man's sense of oneness with nature and other men. No doubt he found in these poems elements of himself and, responding to their affinities with his ideas, collected them with a view to setting them to music.

The remarkable thing is that exactly the same can be said about the writer whose play became the basis for Stevens' one completed opera, J.M. Synge. In setting *The Shadow of the Glen* Stevens' artistic life came full circle, for he had been interested in the Irish playwright from his earliest student years, and it is almost as though the experiments with other writers, forms, and styles were necessary attempts to define the bounds of his creative concern, before he could return to the centre and give it its most concentrated expression; there is, in the fact of his completing this opera at the end of his life, an aspect of wonderful self-realisation.

When he left Cambridge, Stevens went to the Royal College of Music where, among other things, he studied with R.O. Morris. This was at the suggestion of Vaughan Williams who, in 1931, had set to music *Riders to the Sea*, the play Synge wrote immediately before *The Shadow of the Glen*. *Riders* was, in fact, first staged at the College in 1937, while Stevens was studying there.

It is inconceivable that Stevens did not discuss the opera with Vaughan Williams, and that the idea of doing something similar should not have occurred to him then.

As a student of literature, Stevens had an abiding interest in Synge, the more so as Synge himself had also studied both music and literature, taking a BA at Trinity College, Dublin in 1892, and at about the same time a scholarship in harmony and counterpoint at the Royal Irish Academy of Music. He then went on to study music in Germany for a year before 'seeing that the Germans were so much more innately gifted with the musical faculties than I was that I decided to give up music and take to literature instead'. In 1893 Synge had even begun the words and music of an opera on *Eileen Aruin*, and his first literary attempts, according to Professor Ann Saddlemyer, have a tendency towards the exaggerations of romantic opera.

In 1898 Synge went for the first time to the Aran Islands and got to know the inhabitants by sharing their hard life, and to do so the better, by learning their language. There was no romantic idealisation here of the simple life; no sentimental descriptions penned by the light of a drawing-room fire; what he wrote into his plays, he heard sheltering from the Atlantic gale, from the mouths of people who had little, but knew much. And when he dared with exquisite exactitude to represent it faithfully in *The Shadow of the Glen* his bourgeois patrons walked out; but Synge knew the truth of it and would not alter a syllable.

As a student, Stevens would no doubt have respected the rigour of Synge's style; but, as a man who, for some years since 1943, had been a communist, continuing as a strong humanitarian, and had suffered for his beliefs, he profoundly sympathised with the predicament of Synge's characters. As a musician he resonated with the lyricism of Synge's texts.

It was also this lyricism that harnessed his concern and sympathy with the common man. The accident of their similar educations would not have been enough to engage the creative energy of a man as thoroughly high-principled as Stevens. It was their common feeling for the poor and disadvantaged, the simple and natural, the essential and unspoilt, that finally determined him to expend his last energies on such an undertaking. I hope it is not over-romanticising to say that with it his life achieved its purpose and made its statement. *The Shadow of the Glen* is Stevens' personal testimony and his masterpiece.

Having begun work on it in the early 1970s, Stevens was held up by much increased organisational and teaching duties at the RCM and London University. He was eventually granted an Arts Council bursary in November 1978 to finish it, and speedily did so, having learnt by then that he was suffering from malignant cancer.

It was composed mainly in Menorca, with what Bertha Stevens calls pleasurable fluency. A study of the pencil final draft of the short score reveals that much care had gone into the work, nearly every bar having at some stage been erased or altered. Often this appears to be simply for the purpose of making clearer what had already been written. At any rate, he was obviously able to concentrate, and the ideas flowed freely, even if their final form on paper needed more consideration.

He researched his sources thoroughly and owned a copy of Synge's book *The Aran Islands* which Synge considered his 'first serious piece of work – it was written before any of the plays'. It is in this that Synge tells how he first heard the story which so soon became *The Shadow of the Glen*; it was told to him by old Pat Dirane on the middle island of Aran, Inishmaan, in 1898.

> One day I was travelling on foot from Galway to Dublin, and the darkness came on me and I ten miles from the town I was wanting to pass the night in. Then a hard rain began to fall and I was tired walking, so when I saw a sort of a house with no roof on it up against the road, I got in the way the walls would give me shelter.
>
> As I was looking round I saw a light in some trees two perches off, and thinking any sort of a house would be better than where I was, I got over a wall and went up to the house to look in at the window.
>
> I saw a dead man laid on a table, and candles lighted, and a woman watching him. I was frightened when I saw him, but it was raining

hard, and I said to myself, if he was dead he couldn't hurt me. Then I knocked on the door and the woman came and opened it.

'Good evening, ma'am,' says I.

'Good evening kindly, stranger,' says she. 'Come in out of the rain.'

Then she took me in and told me her husband was after dying on her, and she was watching him that night.

'But it's thirsty you'll be, stranger,' says she. 'Come into the parlour.'

Then she took me into the parlour—and it was a fine clean house—and she put a cup, with a saucer under it, on the table before me with fine sugar and bread.

When I'd had a cup of tea I went back into the kitchen where the dead man was lying, and she gave me a fine new pipe off the table with a drop of spirits.

'Stranger,' says she, 'would you be afeard to be alone with himself?'

'Not a bit in the world, ma'am,' says I; 'he that's dead can do no hurt.'

Then she said she wanted to go over and tell the neighbours the way her husband was after dying on her, and she went out and locked the door behind her.

I smoked one pipe, and I leaned out and took another off the table. I was smoking it with my hand on the back of my chair—the way you are yourself this minute, God bless you—and I looking on the dead man, when he opened his eyes as wide as myself and looked at me.

'Don't be afeard, stranger,' said the dead man; 'I'm not dead at all in the world. Come here and help me up and I'll tell you all about it.'

Well, I went up and took the took the sheet off of him, and I saw that he had a fine clean shirt on his body, and fine flannel drawers.

He sat up then, and says he—

'I've got a bad wife, stranger, and I let on to be dead the way I'd catch her goings on.'

Then he got two fine sticks he had to keep down his wife, and he put them at each side of his body, and he laid himself out again as if he was dead.

In half an hour his wife came back and a young man along with her. Well, she gave him his tea, and she told him he was tired, and he would do right to go and lie down in the bedroom.

The young man went in and the woman sat down to watch by the dead man. A while after she got up and 'Stranger,' says she, 'I'm going in to get the candle out of the room; I'm thinking the young man will be asleep by this time.' She went into the bedroom, but the divil a bit of her came back.

Then the dead man got up, and he took one stick, and he gave the other to myself. We went in and we saw them lying together with her head on his arm.

The dead man hit him a blow with the stick so that the blood out of him leapt up and hit the gallery.

That is my story.

Here is the natural source material for Synge's play, which even contains some of the dialogue recorded by the author, which of course finds its way into the opera.

The story teller, Pat Dirane, finds fictional immortality as the Tramp, the young wife as Nora Burke, the old husband as Dan Burke, and the young man as Michael Dara. Synge's play dispensed with the wife going to bed with the young man, and substitutes the theatrically more telling episode when they count her fortune while her husband listens under his shroud, and ends with old Dan sending his wife out of the house to the welcoming arms of the Tramp, while he takes her young lover into partnership on his farm. In the opera Nora Burke becomes a mezzo (Bernadette Greavy was in Stevens' mind as he wrote it), Dan a baritone, The Tramp a bass and Michael a tenor.

The play was produced on 8 October 1903 and, to quote Saddlemyer, whose edition of the plays Stevens owned and worked from, 'with that production the long battle between Synge and the Irish Nationalists began'. It was the realism they couldn't take, and it was the realism that both Synge in his play and Stevens in his opera wanted to underline. It is important to realise that this realism was not the mere 'slice of life' depiction of reality but, in a profounder sense, that by celebrating reality, art becomes reality itself.

Stevens read up the commentaries on this dispute, and owned a rare copy of the monograph *Synge and the Ireland of His Time by William Butler Yeats with a Note Concerning a Walk through Connemara with him by Jack Butler Yeats*, in which some of the threads of the quarrels are untangled.

Synge records in *The Aran Islands* that when Pat Dirane told the story it gave rise to a big argument among the young men, but that as it was conducted in rapid Gaelic he could not follow it all. I imagine the argument would have concerned the rightness or otherwise of the actions of husband and wife, and certainly the arguments the play later gave rise to concerned, at least in part, this aspect.

Stevens himself sympathised passionately with the predicament of the poor, and was a critic of an economic system that cheated people of happiness. In Ireland at that time, as indeed in other peasant economies, a young girl could hope only to be married to an older man who had lived long enough and worked hard enough to amass the means wherewith to support her.

In his copy of the plays Stevens has pencilled in the margin against certain sections of Saddlemyer's introduction, quoting Synge's thoughts, that seemed to him significant. They all concern the reality of the play. He was writing an opera to be staged, and I believe that, as he wrote it, he imagined, as Synge had done, the movements and manners of the people that Synge had wanted to set down, and this was Stevens' starting point; as he set Synge's lines he must have kept in mind the playwright's own thoughts:

> The folk melody is complete in itself; the folk poems need a music which must be drawn from the words by the reader or reciter. In primitive time every poet recited his own poem with the music that he conceived with the words in his moment of excitement. Any of his hearers who admired the work repeated it with the exact music of the poet. This is still done among the Aran islanders. An old man who could not read has drawn tears to my eyes by reciting verse in Gaelic I did not fully understand. The modern poet composes his poems with often extremely subtle and individual intonations which few of his readers ever interpret adequately. . . . I have often thought of a collection of pressed flowers, when listening to ordinary reading dealing with poetry. The flower is there but its perspective and perfume are lost. . . . Sometimes in my MS I have marked all the intonations ff. rall. etc. but it has a certain affectation and what is worse would become mechanical with the reader. . . . Perhaps in a few years a perfected science will render the poet's voice again immortal.

And Stevens probably had an idea of a sound in his head, of a kind of vocal quality that would hint at or suggest what Synge himself records in *The Aran Islands*, and which again Stevens pencils in the margin. Synge recalls how, walking out one day with 'a curious man', a wintry shower drove them to seek shelter, crouching in the bracken under a loose wall. The man sang to him and, wrote Synge, 'the music was much like what I have heard before on these islands – a monotonous chant with pauses on the high and low notes to mark the rhythm; but the harsh nasal tone in which he sang was almost intolerable'.

Not that there is anything harsh, monotonous or intolerable in Stevens' music, but of a chant there is. The whole piece is based on the *Dies Irae* plainsong, expounded at the outset in the only genuinely witty treatment of this much-used theme I know.

The economy of gesture and scale perfectly match the austerity of the *mise en scène*, and allow a flexibility of language which can catch exactly the accents of Synge's song-speech.

The remarkably perspicacious last paragraph of Dent's letter comes to mind once again. Here Stevens' 'austerity of style' found its natural partner and ally; here Synge's poetic naturalism found its expressive vehicle.

The whole musical texture has the feeling of organic growth, and a very natural flow which belies the sustained intellectual effort in organising the material. Melody and accompaniment are spun out of the intervals of the chant, one motif leading seamlessly into another with inexorable logic, always sensitive to the demands of the text.

Stevens prepared his own libretto from the play, setting about half the total text. A glance at his copy of the play shows graphically how the dramatic pacing is achieved so effectively. Stevens has scored out all the lines he does not require, shortening the conversations and tightening up the more extended soliloquies; but this scoring out becomes less frequent towards the end, until the two long paragraphs of the Tramp's lyrical invitation to Nora to join him are left complete, and are set to music which becomes an ecstatic paean to the natural world.

The conversations are carried on in the more *parlando* style sections, and Stevens uses Synge's soliloquies, albeit edited, as the basis for more deeply lyrical sections, more like traditional arias. These are strategically placed throughout the work to heighten interest and tension, each one carrying the drama on to a new peak, until the end when the Tramp, who has had very little opportunity to 'sing out' up to now, launches out on his great hymn to life.

Nora accepts this new life, rejecting the drab 'commercialism' of her loveless marriage, and enters on a new experience of body and soul; for Stevens she must have appeared the epitome of the new heroine of the people, a personification of the creative life suppressed within them.

Stevens' musical technique itself seems to be a metaphor for all this. The materials he uses, like the characters he portrays, are all ordinary enough, plain even, but great riches are spun out from the fabric of the chant, symbolising the life that has to be drawn out of the personalities in the drama if they are to live in their own right. And it is all done so artlessly, with so little apparent effort; the subtle craftmanship maintains its firm hold to the very last. How in the short time he has left to play his opera out could Stevens follow the emotional weight of the Tramp's peroration? The solution is so simple that it passes by, unremarked; simply by permitting himself the only bars of duet singing in the whole piece, as Dan calls the young shepherd, Michael, back to drink with him and the two men toast each other.

And to think all this musical life has been culled from a plainsong chant for the dead! Nothing could better symbolise Stevens' acceptance and positive affirmation of life. Means and message are one; a marriage of true minds, and Stevens realised himself completely.

When he had finished *The Shadow of the Glen* in 1979 Stevens immediately sent the score to the B.B.C., among other organisations, but it wasn't until April 1982 that it was eventually recorded. Della Jones took the role of Nora; Neil Mackie, Michael; John Gibbs, Dan; and Paul Hudson the Tramp. The orchestra was Divertimenti (with Stevens' daughter Cathy in the viola section), and the conductor was Howard Williams. Stevens attended the recording, where he was amused to be told by Della Jones that he had adjudicated a competition she was in when she was a child. He died the following January, however, and although he did hear a tape of the recording, he was never to hear the first broadcast, which took place on Radio 3 on 22 May 1983.

Talking with Messiaen. (Copyright: the Royal College of Music)

Reminiscences

Some Reflections on the Piano Concerto
James Gibb

In February 1982 Bernard wrote to say that he had nearly finished the revision of his Piano Concerto. Some months before he had told me of his plan to re-fashion the work in order to give it a more stringent dramatic unity. To my delight he asked me if I would perform the work when it was completed. I have never seen the score of the original version, but I knew when he was writing it in 1950, that a performance was being considered for the Cheltenham Festival of 1951. With this in view, Sir John Barbirolli asked to see the score, but as Bernard was working on another commission it was not finished in time, and his Sinfonietta was programmed instead. In fact with the intervention of other commissions, the Concerto was not completed until 1955. In the following year, having read the completed score, both Rudolf Schwarz then conductor of the City of Birmingham Symphony Orchestra, and Karl Rankl of the Scottish National Orchestra expressed great admiration for the work, but in the end a performance was not arranged. I heard no mention of the piece by Bernard himself until, all those years later, he expressed his desire to revise it. From time to time he told me of progress on the revision, saying that the solution to his problem was proving simpler than he had at first anticipated. It was not at all my impression that it was undertaken in the spirit of expediency, or that he was patching up old material the better to attract programme planners to accept it. In any case such catch-penny motives were quite foreign to his nature.

Knowing the stage which Bernard's illness had reached, it was a relief to hear in May 1982 that a performance was being planned for December 8th of that year with the BBC Welsh Orchestra. Later, when the contract arrived, we discovered that one of the two rehearsals promised, without any warning to us, had been cancelled because another concert had been scheduled for the day before our recording. After remonstration that one rehearsal would be quite inadequate for a good performance the work was re-scheduled for March 24th 1983. Welcome news, but Bernard's condition cast doubts on any possibility of him surviving long enough to hear the performance of his work. I was very anxious to have his advice and decided to take whatever opportunity there might be over the Christmas holiday. I had been rehearsing it with my friend Mary Peppin playing the orchestral part on a second piano. On New Year's Day we set off on the short journey from Mary's cottage to Great Maplestead. Bertha, herself on the point of exhaustion from her prolonged and devoted night-and-day nursing, had warned us that morning on the telephone that Bernard might not feel well enough to hear us play. As it happened, after some preliminary vagueness, no doubt under the powerful effect of his medication, he said very emphatically that he wanted to hear the Concerto. I had to support him on the short path from the house to the erstwhile blacksmith's forge, now converted to a well-equipped and congenial music studio. Those few yards were physically very painful for him, but, once settled in a chair in the studio with the score we saw again that familiar, full-moon smile of his. In a moment he was his old benign and lucid self. We played straight through the Concerto. At the end a short silence and then out came the words – "Fantastic piece" – a comment as touching as it was, by its sheer unexpectedness, comical. In discussing a few details it became clear to me that he was convinced of the validity of his revision. On request we played the work a second time before he faced the pain of those few yards back to the house. It proved to be his last day at home.

A performer, in preparing a work for performance is usually so intent on realising every virtue it may contain that he is, perforce, inclined to suspend or allay his own critical judgment of the piece while he concentrates on discovering, to the limit of his talent, how much more he can contribute to its presentation. The experience, conscious and subconscious, of an actual performance is the crucial test. After that has taken place the player is in a much better position to trust his own judgment. The performance of the Concerto recorded with the BBC Welsh Orchestra conducted by Brian Wright some three months after Bernard died left me in the full belief that it was a work of unusual power and that it possessed a compelling dramatic unity. From beginning to end it had the stamp of inevitability.

Reflecting on the many years gap between the first version of the Concerto and its revision one is bound to speculate on other factors that might have affected Bernard's career, in general, as a composer. It seems clear now that changes in musical fashion and in musical hierarchies in the 50's had an adverse influence. An increasing amount of time was spent in earning his living as a teacher and examiner. What was not so clear to public view was the effect that Bernard's deeply-held political and philosophical views, his allegiance to Marxism, had on his future. The year 1955, when he completed the Concerto, the Cold War was in full swing. The enormities of Senator McCarthy's anti-communist witch-hunt in America were at their peak. The Senator had his sympathisers in this country, and not only in political circles. In that same year Bernard stood as witness in a slander case which Edward Clark, the President of the International Society for Contemporary Music and husband of the composer, Elisabeth Lutyens, brought against Benjamin Frankel for alleged imputations of having embezzled ISCM funds. The jury's verdict denied proof of slander but added a rider, "Mr. Clark's integrity is not in doubt". However, in the course of the hearing Frankel's lawyers decided unexpectedly to cast a political slur into the case, pointing out that two of Clark's witnesses were members of the Communist Party, and implying that, therefore, they would be prepared, if so instructed, to lie. As Elisabeth Lutyens recorded in her autobiography, *A Goldfish Bowl* – "Two days of the hearing were devoted to the attempt to discredit Edward's honourable witnesses (not too difficult in those days of fear and suspicion) and two days in trying to prove Edward's dishonesty". Not mentioned by name in her book, one of those "honourable witnesses" was, of course, Bernard. Frankel, himself, had been a friend of Bernard's and a fellow-member of the Communist Party but had severed his political allegiance a few years before the case. There is no doubt that the case itself sparked off bitter personal recriminations and added fuel to factional antagonisms that already existed in musical circles. This, together with the switch of musical fashion towards the Second Viennese School and its adherents may have combined to cast a cloud over Bernard's future. Whether or not Bernard was made professionally to suffer for his opinions and that some measure of the neglect of his music can be attributed to hidden acts of discrimination cannot be proved one way or the other. (His music, in any case, demands devoted advocacy to make its mark. He was as incapable of adding any ingratiating gloss to what he had to say in music as he was impatient of such behaviour in life.) Those who, like myself, shared Bernard's views and allegiances came to hear of other cases in which acts of political discrimination actually did take place. Colleagues who were in the position to know and who heartily disapproved of such practices would tell us of them. These discriminatory acts were always covert. The real political motive was never publicly admitted, leaving, I suppose a small modicum of comfort in the thought that the hypocrite, by his very deviousness, is acknowledging the existence and the power of an honourable code of conduct.

Robert Simpson in his Preface has described eloquently and accurately the nature of Bernard's political beliefs, their humanitarian base, and the link between them and his view of the composer's function in society. These remained constant. It was that same constancy that ultimately impelled his resignation from the Communist Party. The events in Hungary in 1956 were only the last straw in a burden that had been gathering an intolerable weight for some considerable time before. Impassioned partisanship may at times have momentarily clouded his vision, but his honest intellectual vigour and vast knowledge assured him freedom from any kind of automatic dogmatism.

In the last weeks of his life his creative imagination was taking a new and original lease of life. In one of our last meetings he talked about composing a setting of a Mexican folk poem about whales. His friend Edward Williams, the composer, had promised to obtain for him recordings of their song, suggestions of which Bernard was hoping to incorporate. The setting was to involve an immense variety of percussion instruments and would represent for him an entirely new venture in instrumental sound. But it was not to be. His going left behind, for all who knew and loved him, a grateful realisation of how much we had all gained from the warmth of his friendship and the always sensitive perceptive guidance we received from his vast knowledge, so lightly worn and so generously dispensed.

II
Bernard Stevens and the University of London
Brian Trowell

I first became aware of Bernard Stevens when I heard his Piano Trio op. 3 (1942) performed at a concert in Big School at Christ's Hospital in 1943 or 1944. Musical tastes at my old school were, and long remained, decidedly conservative, and it was something of an event to hear a work so recently composed. I was then twelve or thirteen, an age when one's reactions are instinctive rather than intellectual; but I remember – since I was then trying to compose – feeling stimulated and encouraged by the trio's passion and energy and firm tonal tread. Here was music undeniably new and individual, which at the same time derived much of its strength from a sense of past traditions. It had style, both in its own inner coherence and consistency, and also in the larger sense of a convention not private to the composer but readily comprehensible to a wider audience as well.

After that, I looked out for Bernard Stevens' name, and picked up a number of performances and broadcasts over the years, of works which it's not my brief to discuss here; they confirmed my boyhood impression of a musical personality that was passionate but not impetuous, classically minded and yet English, subjective and yet concerned to give both performer and listener their due. I learned that their composer was distinctly left-wing; but he resolutely refused, during the 1950s and 60s, that period of extraordinary and bewildering experimentation, to re-think his basic language or climb on to any of the bandwagons offered by avant-garde criticism or the BBC. That does not mean that he turned his back on new ideas: those that interested him he re-worked in his own way, incorporating them into the tonal, thematic and motivic idioms that suited him best. The second String Quartet of 1962 comes to mind, where the integrative devices of serialism become the very clearly audible basis of harmony which flowers into melodic lines, and melodies which contract into harmony.

When I came to the University of London from the BBC in 1970, I was certainly curious to meet Bernard Stevens. University music studies were then still in a state of some uncertainty, for the turmoil created by Thurston Dart's radical new syllabuses for all the London degrees in Music had not fully died down. Their introduction, and the concomitant abandonment of the old London B. Mus. and D. Mus., had led in 1965 to a major walk-out from the Board of Studies in Music (essentially the Faculty's governing body): Herbert Howells, Gordon Jacob, Sidney Watson, Lloyd Webber and Sir Ernest Bullock all resigned, followed a year later by Eric Thiman, and it looked for a time as if the Royal Academy of Music and the Royal College of Music would cease to present students for the University's B. Mus. In 1966 the College pronounced that 'it would be impossible to provide an adequate training at the College for Part II of the [new B. Mus.] syllabus. It seems unlikely therefore that after this year we shall be able to accept students for the degree'.

Dart made one compromise and introduced Composition as a Special Subject in the finals of the B. Mus., but otherwise stuck to his guns. The old London-style academic harmony and counterpoint that had bulked so large in the old B. Mus. were never to return; their place was taken by little more than two terms' study, based on the analysis and imitation of real music, of the period c1575-1830. He was determined to make room in the syllabus for a mass of new material, including a frightening compulsory paper on musical instruments throughout the world, past and present, and many almost interdisciplinary papers on music in different contexts, including jazz. Now the point of all this history of academic in-fighting is that it seems to have been Bernard Stevens, then teaching at the Royal College of Music, who decided that the old London degrees were out of keeping with the new age, and that Dart was a good musician who had earned the right to suggest new ideas but would not be deaf to common sense. He led the way at the Royal College by suggesting that the new ideas should be taken seriously, became a 'recognized teacher' of the University in March 1967 and accordingly joined the Board of Studies in Music; which is where I first met him in 1971.

I was aware of the problems that Dart had faced in relation to the music colleges, and was very green over academic music after eight years outside the university world. Knowing that I might be resented as a Dart pupil, a teacher at King's College and a BBC smoothie, my first sight of Bernard across a committee table filled me with apprehension. Steely grey hair and moustache, a strong firm gaze focussed through steel-rimmed glasses, a florid and uncompromising appearance, and a formal, almost chanted delivery in his 'official' manner of speech: here, I thought at first, was a tough customer.

How wrong I was. Once the meeting was over, and we had all stood up and moved away from the 20ft square of those official boardroom tables, I discovered that the spectacle frames were a delicate silver and the eyes behind them a soft dark brown, sensitive, friendly, sometimes visionary. Bernard proved firm and tough in his convictions alright; but what good and well-tempered convictions they were, realistic and practical, but at the same time imaginative and full of musical and human understanding. And how hard he worked, both at meetings and as an examiner. In the latter capacity he proved extraordinarily learned in all aspects of twentieth-century music; one might have expected that his knowledge and approval would be restricted to fairly traditional composers whose style had something in common with his own (a limitation too often observable, *mutatis mutandis*, in avant-garde composers). But no, he was thoroughly up-to-date and well acquainted with both the techniques and the aesthetic of the most recent experimental music. And if he was asked to advise on something quite outside his normal beat, such as the educational ideas of Orff and Kodaly, he cheerfully set to and learned what was needed, though the fees for examining were derisory when one considered that a music college teacher had to give up paid work in order to undertake the duties.

His contribution was equally remarkable when the University and music colleges got together a little money and, with Arts Council help, put on a three-day festival of difficult new music with open rehearsals, talks, and discussions with the performers. We projected the scores on to large screens by means of transparencies. The original idea came, I think, from Bernard; he was concerned that London B. Mus. students (by now the largest collection of Music students at any British university), who all had to sit an important paper in twentiety-century music, had so little chance in the mid-70s to gain really close experience of it in live performance. It was thanks to Bernard's advocacy that Sir David Willcocks kindly granted us free use of the Concert Hall at the Royal College of Music. The whole thing took a great deal of organising, and Bernard devoted many hours of unpaid time, and a good deal of excellent gin, to make the planning committee's meetings both effective and enjoyable. And here again, his knowledge of recent developments in composition proved invaluable.

It was at this time that I got to know him well, and to relish his sharp eye and ear for the absurd, and the demonic inner glee of his humour (for he seldom laughed aloud). It's a pity that we never had a tape-recorder near, to capture the astonishing stream of reminiscences, with verbatim recall of conversations he had had with distinguished composers of the previous generation, that flowed from his amazingly accurate memory. All I can now recollect is a striking picture of Sorabji in his country cottage, his grand piano covered with manuscripts that he refused to let anyone look at. Let's hope that some of this is set down for posterity in Bernard's unpublished letters and papers.

His services to University music was indeed remarkable, and it was entirely fitting that my musical colleagues wished to honour him by asking him to become Dean of the Faculty of Music. He was surprised and touched, I think; but it was not to be. His health was starting to give him trouble, and he wished to devote his time more to composition and teaching. We understood, but surmised, with apprehension that later proved justified, that his illness might be more serious than he chose to reveal. When his passing was reported to the Board of Studies, and the University's musicians stood in sorrowful silence round that table, our minds were filled with much more than conventional gratitude, and with unusually happy memories of all that Bernard had done for us, and for his and our students.

III
Conversation about Bernard Stevens
John Barstow and Roderick Swanston

JB The first time I ever met Bernard Stevens, or even heard of him, and this is where in a peculiar way my respect for him started, I was doing an Associated Board exam in Leeds. I arrived early, you know how it is with your mother patting you on the head and your gloves on, to find that the candidate before me hadn't turned up. Bernard Stevens appeared at the door of the examination room and said, 'Are you the next one?' 'Yes', I replied. 'You can come in now', he added in that unique voice, which had to be heard to be believed (but which certainly can't be written down); and as I passed him to enter the room he said, almost as though he were really only talking to himself, 'I hope you can play, because none of them so far this morning has been able to play at all'. It was devastating – at any rate at that age. Anyway I got a distinction, but only just, since the report form showed clearly he had put me up from 128 to 130. He must have been desperate.

But it made its impression, because when I came to the Royal College of Music and I was looking for someone to teach me composition as a second study I felt automatically drawn to ask for him, and I never regretted it. Throughout the entire time I learnt with him he always related my composition work to my piano work. For instance, when I was doing orchestration, he made me orchestrate a book of Debussy *Preludes* because he felt that this would help me to add colour to my playing of them. He also felt that most people didn't play them with enough colour – and he was right!

In his lessons he also wanted to extend me as a person. For instance when he found out what my interests were he decided I needed to do some sixteenth century counterpoint because I had never done anything like it before. And he taught it not as a dead exercise, but so that I could experience its rhythmic freedom. He spent a lot of time talking about plainsong and about music in general instead of just pushing Bach chorales at me.

He was very clever at relating to what I was working at on the piano. When I was going to do the Bartók Suite, he said, 'Always keep a Bartók quartet in your pocket', and then in the lessons he would talk about both, and show me how they were connected and how one would help me learn the other. And when we got on to freeish composition he said 'Why don't you write cadenzas for the first four Beethoven concertos?' I replied that I'd only played numbers one and three. 'Well,' he said, 'they're quite easy to get. You know, the library's full of copies. Just get them and learn them, and then write cadenzas for them. There's no mystery about it. You can't object when the music's there. Just because you haven't bothered to find out'. Really blunt and matter-of-fact. Just like that!

I think it was my northernness which responded to that down-to-earthness in him. I suppose in a way he could be thought of as intolerant, but it wasn't really that. It was just that he didn't suffer fools gladly and was much cleverer than a lot of other people.

RS Yes, it was that uncompromising standard he set in his teaching. You know, he was always referring to the story about Webern conducting the Berg *Violin Concerto* in Spain, or somewhere, when the orchestra complained that he was impractical because he spent something like two hours on the first two pages. But Bernard always said it was the orchestra that was unrealistic since it thought it could do it in less.

JB Yes, that's just it. You know in lessons it didn't matter how little you'd done for him, he always used to say, 'Just bring me something as a starting point.' That's how I got to know the Shostakovich *Preludes and Fugues*. They'd just come out and he was full of them. They seemed to him super piano music; piano music that was really pianistic. In those days people like Stockhausen weren't quite so obviously around, so one could still feel that traditionally notated music was the latest thing. Anyway I think Bernard liked Shostakovich because he was a traditionalist himself, though with a very individual voice. He also didn't like to push one to an extreme and he knew that the most contemporary thing I had heard in Leeds was a Mahler symphony. Well, the outcome of his enthusing over the *Preludes and Fugues* was that I went out and bought nearly all I could of Shostakovich; such things as the Piano Trio.

We didn't talk an awful lot in his lessons about his works and I was especially sorry we never looked at his songs. Actually I never tried writing any myself, so perhaps that's why. But it was a pity because when I discovered his later, I found they were beautiful. One work I did get to know was his *Second Ballad*. He asked me if I would like to learn it.

As my piano studies got more demanding and I was spending more and more time on them, it became necessary for me to give up composition and only do theory with Bernard. I must say, nothing changed. He showed just the same interest in me and what I was doing. Whenever I saw him he wanted to know what was going on and why. And when I first tried to study abroad – it happened to be Moscow that I wanted to go to – he was very keen and wrote a very helpful reference for me.

RS He was the most open teacher I can remember, which must have come from his socialist or humanitarian principles. I remember he once showed me the report he had written about me at the end of the year and asked if I thought it was alright. He even said he would change some of it if I thought it wasn't fair. Of course it was, though I don't think it was all that flattering. But it was certainly fair and perceptive. What was he like as a pianist?

JB I think when he was younger he played the piano very well, and in my composition lessons everything he played at the piano was always sensitive and fairly accurate. Sometimes he sent in deputies who couldn't play the piano at all, not even a simple Bach chorale. And this meant that there wasn't really any musical or aural contact in the lesson. It was too abstract. I'd much rather they'd made some stammering attempt. It was quite different with Bernard. Everything he played made sense. Even when he was playing plainsong he managed to suggest its freedom and played as though it was being sung. He was always going on about the sense of music, how it had to communicate its form as well as its sound, and I found this very helpful, since my piano teacher said little about these things.

Bernard was also modest in things that mattered and quite soon he treated me not like a student but like a fellow professional. I remember one occasion when he was going abroad to examine for the Associated Board and was scheduled to give a recital while he was away. He'd decided to play the Britten *Notturno* and came to ask me about fingering some tricky passage – probably those repeated notes in the left hand. It seemed as though we had gone full circle and now I was teaching him, but at the time it didn't seem like that at all. It just seemed like one musician asking another for some practical advice.

RS That's right. In lessons he treated you like an equal and would talk about anything at great length and with a lot of insight. Discussions with him were much more like discussions with a more knowledgeable friend than with a teacher. He would discuss anything freely and frankly, and if he was interested he seemed to lose all sense of time. I remember he would often be so interested in a subject that he wouldn't notice the next student come in. Sometimes this got so bad that there would be a queue of students waiting for lessons as he got more and more behind time. Then he would just look at them, ask them if they had done anything and teach them all together for about ten minutes! If he liked you he never seemed to mind how long lessons went on.

JB I remember he had a very quick wit. One morning he was coming to College and met Philip Wilkinson, who is a keen walker and rock climber, in his kit walking away from College. Bernard asked him if he was going home already (it was only about 8.30 in the morning). Philip said no, he was just going for some climbing practice in Kensington Gardens. 'What, scaling the north face of the Albert Memorial?' came back Bernard with an absolutely straight face.

He also couldn't bear loosely used language. He always used to say he couldn't understand what people meant when they used the word 'musical' in their reports. You know the sort of thing – 'This candidate was not musical.' 'What do they mean?' asked Bernard. 'If you kick them they won't sound A?' What of course he meant was that when his colleagues used the word 'musical' they hadn't bothered to work out what they meant.

RS Yes, that's right. He also didn't mind to whom he said things. He could be devastating in attack. I remember once a very famous violinist came to the College to give a lecture–recital and ended by playing some unaccompanied Bach not at all well. After he had played, the assembled staff and students were invited to ask questions, and a few rather sycophantic questions were put to general approbation. Then Bernard piped up from the back of hall and asked if this famous violinist had tried playing Bach on a baroque violin. No, said the violinist, he felt that his modernised

Strad was more expressive; and he certainly looked as though
the question wasn't worthy of much consideration. So Bernard
charged in with a follow-up, 'Don't you think it might be easier,
though, to get that difficult middle section that crosses strings so
awkwardly, better in tune if you played a baroque instrument?' Well,
the consternation of the violinist was nothing to the sharp intake
of breath from the Director and other professors, who accused
Bernard afterwards of being rude. But he was unrepentant and
simply said that he thought it was a perfectly reasonable question
and couldn't understand why no one else had asked it. He was
certainly not going to take people at their own estimation, and he
also thought in an unpretentious way that an educational institution
should be concerned with truth, not *politesse*.

JB He could be like that when he questioned you in lessons.
I remember once Glenn Gould had given a rather strange
performance of Beethoven's first piano concerto, and I said I
understood Gould had written a 'twelve-note' cadenza.

'That doesn't surprise me at all. Does it you?'

'Well,' I said, 'yes, it sounded funny.'

'What d'yer mean funny? Did you laugh at it?'

'Well, no, it sounded odd.'

'Odd. What d'yer mean, odd? Odd isn't the same thing as
funny. Do you mean strange, unsuitable?'

'Yes'.

'What do you think the cadenza's for then?'

'I don't know. Isn't it the place where the performer exhibits
his technical skill?'

'Well, does that have to be in the period in which the work was
written? Couldn't it reflect the skill of the performer in the time
he was playing it, rather than when the work was written?'

After that I wanted to go away and write a 'twelve-note'
cadenza! I don't think what he said was right, but his way of
asking provocative questions made you think all the time. He also
didn't have any small talk. If you talked with him it was always
about something, and you always needed to think.

RS Do you remember anything more about his enthusiasms in
lessons?

JB Yes. It's more about Shostakovich. When Stokowski came over
from America to conduct Shostakovich's *Fifth Symphony* there was
a lot of fuss. I'd never heard it before but Bernard made it live for

me and was the first to point out the bombast of the finale after
the struggle of the first movement and the serenity of the third.
It didn't matter what you asked, he seemed to know something
about it. You see he also told me something about Stokowski's
background as well. How he had played at St James' Piccadilly and
how he was not just a white-haired showman but a considerable
musician who had done a lot for music.

Later, when the *Fourteenth Symphony* came out, I'd managed to
get a score before he had, so he borrowed mine. He was very
impressed with it.

RS I'm sure he identified with Shostakovich, because you can't
understand Shostakovich without understanding the life of the man
and his reaction to the Soviet state, that is, his changing attitudes
and its changing attitudes. And the fact that the works didn't come
from any kind of clever, intellectual exercise but from real, human
experience. I think all Bernard's work seemed to come from that
too. It was never just a clever exercise.

JB He described, when he was talking about the *Fifth Symphony*
and was mentioning various hallmarks of Shostakovich's style,
how difficult it is to build tension in music, and that quite often
Shostakovich had turned music upside down. When the music was
at its most intense he'd often have strings and piccolos screeching
away at the top of their registers, like the moment in the *Fifth's*
finale when the strings just take off.

Later, when I played the *D minor Prelude and Fugue* at a concert
in the Purcell Room he came round afterwards and said, 'Did you
notice that similarity with the *Fifth Symphony* of the *Prelude and
Fugue.*' Actually I hadn't, but as soon as he said it I realised what
he meant.

RS I remember his talking about Byrd and Purcell in connection
with some lessons he'd heard about someone having with
Hindemith. Hindemith was a composer whom he'd obviously
liked once but who now seemed to have feet of clay. The
person Bernard remembered had been studying some Palestrina
with Hindemith, and had been invited to work out something
like it for the following week. Instead of Palestrina, however, he
decided to work on some Byrd, but Hindemith didn't really know
any Byrd and was contemptuous of him since he was an English
composer, or at any rate that's what Bernard's friend thought he
meant. Neither Bernard nor his friend, of course, took

Hindemith's criticism seriously. In fact Bernard was quite scornful of it. I think he felt that all Hindemith was interested in was bland correctness, not life or individuality.

He also talked about Hindemith in relation to his *Ludus Tonalis*. I was learning to play some of it at the time and he talked about it in the lesson. He said he didn't really understand why the last movement is a retrograde version of the opening. He didn't think you could hear this, so what was the point? 'It might just as well be forwards,' he said. In fact he was a devotee of early Hindemith and told me to get to know *Marienleben* in the early version if I could get hold of a copy. I could only get hold of the later version, but I did go out and buy it on his recommendation and when I showed it to him at the next lesson he was very enthusiastic and talked about it and the differences between the two versions.

JB That's just how it would happen. In my first few lessons he told me to go out and buy the Bartók quartets and *Ludus Tonalis* and R.O. Morris' book on sixteenth century counterpoint, which he regarded as fundamental works with which to start.

RS Bringing us almost back to where you started, did you ever examine with Bernard?

JB Yes, and I remember some very funny things happening there too. When he examined for the ARCM in Schools Music he would always play the devil's advocate. If the candidate said in his exam that there shouldn't be any jazz in his school, Bernard would ask why not. But if he said there should be, Bernard would always ask very belligerently why. Just to test if they had thought about it. I remember sometimes he looked as though he was dozing off in exams, but actually he was listening very carefully, and would sometimes surprise a candidate, and the other examiners for that matter, with a quick pertinent question. Once one of the examiners asked the candidate if he would like to do some sight-reading. 'Oh no, not more sight-reading. Haven't we had enough already?' Bernard was heard to say in a clearly audible exam whisper! In fact on one occasion a candidate was playing particularly badly and Bernard almost cried out, 'Stop her! stop her! For God's sake stop her!' I suppose it was part of his honesty and sincerity that made him do these things, which could seem rude but actually seemed quite appropriate comments for him to make. It was all part of the man.

Oddly enough, there's another incident I remember well which

is the same sort of thing. I remember having a lesson first thing
in the morning and arriving a little before him, so we went to his
room together. When he'd opened the door there was a terrible
smell of silicone polish. He was horrified and flung the door wide
open as well as the windows. I was surprised and said, 'Whatever's
the matter? It's cold.' But he retorted, 'I read a newspaper article
yesterday that said that a woman had killed her baby accidentally
by leaving an open tin of polish next to the pram. I'm not going
to die just for the cleanliness of this building'. So we had to go for
a walk until the smell in the room had cleared. In fact we didn't
go back all morning.

RS How would you sum up your experience of Bernard?

JB Well, the more you speak, the more it comes back. I suppose
it was that interest in everything one was doing, and that ability
to find something important to say about it, something that would
help to get deeper into it.

RS Yes, it was that integrity, that interest and that wit. He was
always looking for the ridiculous side of things, since he valued
serious things so much. He always managed to see a different
angle on things and put them in a new context. It was his way of
cherishing them. Learning with him was fun and inspiring.

IV
Teacher and Friend
Malcolm Lipkin

I first met Bernard at a concert in London, in 1950, and I was immediately struck by his independence of spirit and wide musical tastes. I had just entered the Royal College of Music after having attended several Summer Schools of Music at Bryanston, where I had heard unfamiliar works by Stravinsky, Bartók and Schoenberg, then very little played. I quickly realized that, after Bryanston, the College generated a stifling atmosphere in which interest in recent music was very slight, and which encouraged a backward-looking attitude among many students that I found deplorable. To my kindly professor of 'theory' my music was 'just Bartók', and I longed for a release from such an inhibiting outlook.

It was at this juncture that I remembered Bernard, who was also teaching at the College. After being at first unsuccessful in trying to become one of his pupils, the College authorities eventually placed me with him. I was never officially a composition pupil, for our main work was on theory and counterpoint. However, it was not long before he was looking at my new pieces, with an eagerness which I later found to be so characteristic. During my period of study, which lasted from 1951 to 1953, we discussed virtually every kind of music, and I particularly appreciated his dry sense of humour, especially when castigating music which he did not very much like!

After I left the College, we remained firm friends, meeting from time to time, occasionally in unexpected places. In 1968 we found ourselves in Port Elizabeth, South Africa, sitting next to each other at a concert which included Beethoven's Fourth Piano Concerto. The unexpected sounds of an apple train locomotive, shunting in a nearby goods yard, proved a hilarious accompaniment to Beethoven's slow movement, reducing the dramatic dialogue between piano and orchestra to a farce which had us in fits of laughter.

I was deeply saddened by his untimely death and I shall always remember him with affection.

V

A Reminiscence of my teacher
Michael Finnissy

I first met Bernard Stevens in 1963, when I went to study at the Royal College of Music in London. In spite of having studied, impatiently, with a whole succession of local piano teachers, Stevens was the first composer I'd met, and the first person with whom I'd studied composition. As it happened, meeting him was rather more by luck than by judgment: I had applied to study with Peter Racine Fricker (a former colleague of my last local piano teacher) and, in the event, Fricker was on leave, and so I was 'assigned' to Dr Stevens. In the minds of the RCM students, certain teachers were by reputation terrifying and others much much gentler. On this scale Stevens was most definitely an ogre. In retrospect I can better understand why he had acquired this completely undeserved reputation: unappreciative of his real qualities, the RCM. had, for years, assigned him 'harmony and counterpoint' students, and – admittedly – composition students are (doubtless fortunately) in shorter supply, but I think that he was becoming extremely frustrated that with all the wisdom and knowledge he had to pass on, none of the 'h. and c.' dimwits could've cared less. Thus he could, with justification, be severely critical of their half-hearted and pathetic efforts, and I think it was almost with relief that he found someone who wanted to be a composer, rather than a music teacher.

In fact I was not the only student then studying with him who had this aspiration towards 'real' composition. The very first words I heard him speak, whilst cowering outside his door prior to our first meeting, were alternately shouted lacerations and whispered pinpricks of language very definitely in angry criticism of a fellow student composer (Peter Klatzow), and as I listened on, the unfortunate Klatzow tried to defend himself by evoking Sibelius; this brought a surprising reaction from the imagined ogre – there was a swift peal of blustery laughter and then a much kinder murmuring of voices, at which point – ten or fifteen minutes after Klatzow's lesson was supposed to end and mine begin – I knocked on the door and went in.

Most people who are taught, and go on to teach, have some notion of what constitutes a really good teacher. In the case of the creative arts good teachers are very rare: the degree of self-sacrifice and the buoyancy of energy and commitment required eliminate almost everyone. Stevens was, quite unequivocally, one of the rarest of the rare ones – but, undoubtedly, at great cost to his career as composer.

Studying with him was like exploring; whatever the departure point, there were always fascinating and invigorating things to discover. Some of the points of departure were dictated by the College curriculum: Palestrina-style counterpoint, Bach-fugue and so on. For Palestrina-style there was also a prescribed book, by R.O. Morris, and never having had any formal training before, I was incompetent and at a loss. Stevens then articulated, painstakingly and in the most penetratingly imaginative way, how all counterpoint functioned, how it breathed, how it tensed and relaxed, and somehow made it all the most natural and stimulating thing imaginable. By explaining these general principles he made counterpoint – hitherto an intimidating word – alive, useful, and valuable, a concept one used without overtly thinking about it, in short, very practical. In discussing Bach we encountered Purcell and Dowland. I was passionate, and still am, about Purcell; Stevens was passionate about Dowland, and he neither disguised this, nor forced it when he realised that I wasn't. This was another special gift: to share his student's enthusiasms and expand them, without insisting on any supremacy or hierarchical ordering of composers. I used to take delight in challenging his apparently inexhaustible expertise, but from Alkan to Bernd-Alois Zimmermann, via Hába, Mossolov and Nono, everything was bubbling away somewhere in his head. We didn't only discuss music, either; he also had a wealth of information about literature, painting and the theatre, and was unfailingly interested in whatever exhibitions, curios, or dramatic spectacles (this was the era of Genet, Artaud, and 'happenings') I had witnessed.

I am remembering affectionately, of course, and this reminiscence has avoided whatever occasional disagreements and trouble-spots there were; I honestly don't remember many, but I suspect that I was a rather poor student academically, whatever fund of imagination I had, though if Stevens was quite rightly irritated or disappointed by my lack of strict academic accomplishment he never let it show. I was sorry, too, that by the time I was a third-year student and knew him a bit better, he consistently avoided discussion of his own work; he seemed intensely private and secretive about it, and the only allusion I clearly remember is a rather dramatic outburst about what he called an 'almost lost' generation of British composers, who were being overlooked and wrongly assessed. I think he felt neglected and passed over; he needed to be taken seriously, not least because he had an essential seriousness of purpose in his own work, and on the whole he considered jokiness and frivolity in consideration of Art insulting and meaningless. I liked and especially admired him, and I revere his memory.

VI

A Personal Memoir
George Braithwaite

I had known Bernard Stevens since we were at school together in the 1920s, and his untimely death was a great shock. Southend High School for Boys, like so many grammar schools of that period, had no great musical tradition, but there were still many opportunities, and interest in music as a subject was growing, although not yet accepted as an 'academic' subject worthy of serious study.

I have always had a great interest in music, and it was through this that I first remember Bernard as the chap who used to play the organ for morning assembly. The organ, built in memory of the pupils who died in the first World War, was the pride of the school.

I remember Bernard in those early days as a serious boy who lived with his parents in a large, rambling Victorian house near the school, now long since replaced by blocks of offices. He was being taught the piano by a lady I never met, but who clearly was the local Fanny Waterman. She must have been a good teacher, as I clearly remember going to his house when he was 13 or 14 and being greatly impressed by his playing of the Franck *Prelude, Chorale and Fugue* and the *Symphonic Variations*.

Our closer friendship began when a party from the school went to Dunkerque for three weeks during the summer vacation. One of my earliest memories of him is during that trip, when I found him raising the dust from a very old upright piano with a spirited performance of the most famous Chopin polonaise in a classroom in the somewhat decrepit Collège Jean Bart where we were lodged.

Even in those early school days the outwardly serious Bernard sometimes showed the very special sense of ironic humour which I came to know so well later. It was the custom at the school to conclude morning assembly with a voluntary on the organ. Films at that time were preceded by 'Pathé news' at local cinemas and the accompanying cinema organ music always finished with a sequence of rather trite chords played with full vibrato on the

reeds. One morning Bernard finished his voluntary with an exact replica of this effect – to the great disapproval of the Headmaster. The following day Bernard chose a subdued and deliberately sentimental rendering of the opening of Handel's *Xerxes* – then popularly known as *Handel's Largo* – using narrow scale reeds and swell. I can see now the large beaming face of the Headmaster peering down approvingly from the platform, saying 'You played that good, boy, this morning'.

About that time the music master, Percival Small, who bore a remarkable resemblance to Groucho Marx, won a football pool, and gave up the formidable task of trying to teach a 'minor' subject to irreverent boys. His place was taken by Arthur Hutchings, who later became Professor of Music at Durham University. The budget for music was pitifully small, but under Hutchings music began to increase in importance. The school boasted but one ancient upright piano, and I remember Bernard accompanying Hutchings to plead with the Headmaster for a replacement.

The case was put forcibly but the Head remained unmoved. He peered at the music master over half-moon glasses and said ponderously 'That may be as may be . . .'. Hutchings returned to the attack. 'It may *well* be' he said angrily 'that that may be as may be . . . but . . .' To the credit of the Head it must be added that the piano was replaced.

I went up to Trinity Hall, Cambridge in 1933, and Bernard, a year younger than I, followed to St. Johns in 1934. We both read for the English Tripos Part 1 and often attended the same lectures. I well remember going with him to a series of evening lectures by Quiller-Couch. We sat on the floor in the great man's rooms while he discoursed at length over coffee.

Cambridge in the thirties was still the haunt of eccentrics, and we attended lectures by Mansfield Forbes — 'Manny' — to the students. He was supposed to lecture to us on the subject of 'Wordsworth and the Romantics' but, having a personal passion for Scottish architecture, he never, to my recollection, left that subject during the lectures.

Those were the days, too, of the great battle in the English faculty between the romantic A.E. Housman and the highly critical F.R. Leavis. One of the Leavis disciples was I.A. Richards, author of *Practical Criticism*, who lectured to us on the subject of Aristotle's 'ethos' – the principle of ideal excellence. He turned up at the first

lecture bearing a single yellow daffodil which he placed carefully in
front of him on the rostrum. Whether or not he remembered the
report of Oscar Wilde arriving to give a lecture in America carrying
a single white lily, Bernard and I never knew, but at the second
lecture all the undergraduates arrived – each reverently carrying a
yellow daffodil.

One summer evening Bernard and I took a punt for the annual
festival of madrigals performed each year on the river by the
Cambridge University Musical Society, conducted by Boris Ord.
It was the first occasion that it was being broadcast. The custom
was always to finish when it was getting dark with a performance
of 'Draw on Sweet Night'. The singers lit lanterns and their float
of punts was cast off and drifted slowly down river from King's
bridge. As it progressed we heard a burst of laughter spreading
down the banks. It reached us and we saw the cause. The King's
boat club hearties had rounded up hundreds of chamber pots, and
tying them together with string each with a nightlight inside, had
fixed them to the back of the punts without being discovered.
Understandably Boris was not amused!

I went on to read Law, and Bernard took a Mus B. We often
used to repair to a café in the evening to discuss music. I say
'discuss', but it was usually more like a Socratic dialogue, with
myself cast as the enquiring Plato. Even in those days, Bernard's
interests were wide, and there were few subjects in which he could
not more than hold his own.

I had at this time begun to learn the oboe and Bernard, not to
be outdone, bought a bassoon, and after a few weeks we used to
attempt simple works for wind. We met in his rooms to practise.
On one occasion I was climbing the stairs carrying the oboe case.
Above could be heard the strange noises of Bernard practising. I
passed an undergraduate who, glancing at the oboe case said 'Are
you the doctor?'

My diary for this period is littered with references to occasions
of the usual undergraduate type which I attended with him, but
two stand out distinctly in my memory. The first was of going to
the old Guildhall to hear a recital by Stravinsky and Dushkin – an
historic occasion.

The second was when Harold Samuel gave a Bach recital by
candlelight in the old common room at Queens' in May 1935.
Bernard knew Harold Samuel who had given him piano lessons,

and so, after a wonderful performance, we stayed on after the others had left, talking to him round the piano. I well remember the old man holding forth on the need to develop complete independence on the hands in playing Bach. To illustrate this he sat on a low stool with his back to the keyboard and, putting his hands over his shoulders, played a short fugue almost perfectly!

Bernard studied with E.J. Dent and Cyril Rootham, to whom he always admitted a great debt. Vaughan Williams was also associated with the faculty, and I went with Bernard to the first performance of *The Poisoned Kiss* at the Arts Theatre.

A last memory of the Cambridge days was when I listened with him in his rooms to the first broadcast performance of three movements of Walton's first symphony in the summer of 1935. He had a small radio which at one point in the work gave a large flash and emitted smoke. Quite unperturbed, Bernard gave me a quizzical look and remarked with a grin 'It does that sometimes'.

He graduated in music a year after I came down. After Cambridge I kept in touch, but saw him only occasionally. When the war came I joined the Navy, and Bernard, on leaving the Royal College where he had been doing post-graduate studies, joined the Army Pay Corps and was billeted at first in London during the 1940 blitz. He still managed to compose at night, with light music playing to blank out the noise of the ack-ack.

After the War when Bernard and Bertha were married and he was demobilised they lived in Chelsea. Later they bought the violinist Max Rostal's house in Belsize Park, which had a small studio at the end of the garden. But after two years, they escaped the noise and pressures of London, and moved to a delightful cottage in the North Essex countryside, where they remained. Here they joined an ever-widening group of friends – artists, composers and writers. Their daughter Catherine was born two years later.

Bertha was, and is still, a fine orchestral violin player. Always active in her own right, she has done magnificent work in teaching, and in encouraging amateur players by organising and conducting a good amateur orchestra in Suffolk. Their daughter, Cathy, has inherited her parents' talent and has a career as a fine and sensitive viola player.

After the London days we met from time to time, often at performances of Bernard's work in London and elsewhere. Bernard remained unchanged. I remember being with him in Chelsea Town

Hall when the programme included a performance of a work of his based on an Elizabethan theme. Sitting behind us was one of the Chelsea set, studying the programme.

'I see' he said, very audibly 'we have a new work – using someone else's theme . . . why on earth can't these modern chaps write their own themes?' Bernard grinned at me. After the item was over he was invited to the platform to acknowledge the applause. Back in his seat, a hand was placed on his shoulder. 'I say, old chap, I'm frightfully sorry . . . I didn't know . . .'. Bernard turned, and with a very straight face surveyed him. 'Not at all' he said, tongue in cheek, 'I'm rather inclined to agree with you'.

Bernard always wrote with great integrity and never threw off the casual popular piece. At another performance of one of his works which perhaps was not immediately accessible to the ear, a similar voice behind loudly declared 'The trouble with these modern chaps is that they've got no soul'. Bernard looked at me with an owl-like expression of mock seriousness. 'So that's what's the matter with me – I've often wondered . . . got no soul'. The familiar grin followed.

As the years passed, the impressive list of works grew. I was living not too far away and we often met. He always encouraged me in my amateur hobby of making harpsichords and chamber organs, and his advice was always practical and to the point. I often encountered younger people in the musical world who either knew him well or had been students of his at the Royal College of Music. They always spoke with great respect of him and often with affection – especially the students.

He had an insatiable curiosity in every subject and retained to the end wide interests in fields other than music. He was always ready to help and showed great interest in what others were doing. His intolerance of pretension and pomposity sometimes caused friction, I believe, and his ready wit could at times be very caustic.

He had a very special sense of humour which I first experienced when we used to go together to see the Marx Brothers' films when they first came out. Only once did I misjudge it. He had been taking the manuscript score of his Horn Trio to London, and had to change trains. Waiting for the connection, he had been standing too near to the edge of the platform when an express came through and scattered the precious manuscript down the line. I had occasionally done legal work for him and he wrote asking my advice on sueing British Rail: 'What can I do about this sort of thing?' the letter asked. Knowing the chances of legal action were slim, I replied rather flippantly, 'I suggest you don't stand too near the edge of the platform next time'. Bernard, understandably, was not amused.

Illness came upon him suddenly and lasted six years. Few of his friends knew how serious it was going to be. I saw him on several occasions and he never complained – he was always ready to discuss his latest work and remained cheerful and optimistic.

The last time I saw him was in a convalescent home near Colchester. He was sitting up, working on the piece for two pianos and percussion, which he never finished. He also discussed his ideas for writing a Requiem. We talked for quite a while, and when my wife and I left he accompanied us to the top of the stairs. My last, sad memory is of a cheery wave and that half-mischievous smile which I had known since his early teens.

I hate funerals. They can so often be impersonal and formal. But the gathering that fine January afternoon in 1983 was quite different. Bernard had never been a religious person in the formal sense, except for a time as an Anglo-Catholic while at Cambridge, and this simple farewell ceremony in the small parish church at Great Maplestead was a most moving experience.

An intelligent and sensitive Vicar, in consultation with Bertha and Cathy, had agreed to omit the customary formalities, and at their suggestion read from the writings of Teilhard de Chardin. After a fitting and sincere eulogy by a close friend, Edwin Roxburgh, Bertha read an extract from the writings of the Indian holy man Sai Baba, and John Donne's finest sonnet 'Death, be not proud' which Bernard had set in 1981 when asked by the Teilhard Society for a work to be performed at the concert at St. John's Smith Square celebrating the centenary of the birth of Teilhard de Chardin. Nicholas Danby played his organ transcription of Bernard's Elegiac Fugue, and Cathy played beautifully a transcription of the first movement of Bach's D minor cello suite.

The short ceremony finished as simply as it had begun, and we, with many of his friends, filed out into the pale winter sunshine to make our last farewell.

It is a privilege not many of us have to leave a legacy of so much fine work. Bernard's work will be played in future more and more as its sincerity and integrity become more widely appreciated.

Nothing could have been more apt than the last line of that Donne sonnet which Bernard had so recently set, which took me back to those early Cambridge days:

'And Death shall be no more; Death, thou shalt die'.

Notes on the Contributors

JOHN BARSTOW Pianist and teacher. Professor of piano at Royal College of Music. Pupil of Bernard Stevens at R.C.M.

GEORGE BRAITHWAITE Lifelong friend of Bernard Stevens. Lawyer by profession, but a keen amateur musician and instrument-maker.

ALAN BUSH Composer, lecturer and pianist. Professor of composition at Royal Academy of Music 1925-1978. Visiting professor at Berlin and Weimar Hohschüllen. President of the Workers' Music Association and conductor of its Singers from 1944-1956.

MICHAEL FINNISSY Composer and pianist. Pupil of Bernard Stevens at Royal College of Music.

JAMES GIBB Pianist and broadcaster. Head of keyboard department at Guildhall School of Music and Drama.

STEPHEN JOHNSON Writer, broadcaster and music critic.

MALCOLM LIPKIN Composer, pianist and lecturer. Pupil of Bernard Stevens at Royal College of Music.

MALCOLM MACDONALD Writer, composer and broadcaster. Editor of *Tempo* magazine. Author of books on Havergal Brian, John Foulds, Schönberg and others.

WILFRID MELLERS Writer, musicologist and composer. First Professor of Music at York University. Author of books on Couperin, American Music and other subjects. Cambridge contemporary of Bernard Stevens.

HARRY NEWSTONE Conductor. Has conducted many leading orchestras in Europe and the United States and for the BBC.

WILLIAM PLEETH Cellist and teacher. Renowned as performer and conductor of master classes. Author of *The Cello*. Dedicatee of Bernard Stevens's *Cello Concerto*.

MAX ROSTAL Violinist. Professor at Guildhall School of Music and Drama and at Berne and Cologne conservatoires. Dedicatee of Bernard Stevens's *Violin Concerto*.

EDWIN ROXBURGH Composer, conductor and oboist. Director of 20th Century Music department at RCM since 1967 and a professor of composition.

ROBERT SIMPSON Composer, author and BBC producer from 1951-1980. Author of books on Bruckner, Nielsen, Sibelius and others.

CHRISTOPHER de SOUZA BBC producer (especially of opera), lecturer, writer and composer.

BERTHA STEVENS Widow of Bernard Stevens, and mother of Catherine Stevens. Violinist and professor at Royal College of Music from 1969-1981.

RONALD STEVENSON Composer, author, pianist and lecturer. Author of a book on Busoni. Performs his own large-scale works and has given premières of piano works of Bernard Stevens.

RODERICK SWANSTON Lecturer, broadcaster, writer and musicologist. Professor at Royal College of Music since 1976. Pupil of Bernard Stevens at Royal College of Music. Took over Bernard Stevens's teaching on the London BMus course at RCM (as Bernard Stevens did from his teacher, R.O. Morris).

BRIAN TROWELL Musicologist, lecturer, translator, writer and broadcaster. King Edward Professor of Music at King's College, London, from 1974. Heather Professor of Music at Oxford University from 1988.

Discography

NSA is the prefix for recordings held at the British Library National Sound Archive (29 Exhibition Road, London SW7).

BMIC refers to the British Music Information Centre (10 Stratford Place, London W1).

Dates for radio broadcasts are of transmission rather than of recording.

Copies of the four released recordings at the head of this list are also held at the National Sound Archive and British Music Information Centre.

Birthday Song for piano duet, in *Parlour Pieces*

    Isabel Beyer and Harvey Dagul   FHMC 842/1984
    Four Hands Music   Cassette

Cello Concerto and Symphony No 1 *A Symphony of Liberation*

    Alexander Baillie/Edward Downes/   CDE 84124
    BBC Philharmonic. Meridian Records   KE 77124/1987

Theme and Variations and Fuga alla Sarabanda for piano

    Richard Deering/Musica Nova   CD Nova 9
                                 Cassette

Theme and Variations (Quartet No 1) and Quartet No 2., *Lyric Suite* for string trio, and Improvisation for solo viola.

    Delme String Quartet and Catherine Stevens.
    To be released 1989/90

Violin Concerto and Symphony No. 2

    Ernst Kovacic/Edward Downes/BBC Philharmonic CDE 84174
    Meridian Records. To be released 1989   KE 77174

Adagio and Fugue for wind band (1959)

    RNCM Wind Band/Clark Rundell   NSA C345
    Royal Northern College of Music, first   and BMIC
       performance 5/10/85

Autumn Sequence for guitar and harpsichord (1980)

    Raymond Burley (gtr) Stephen Bell (hpsd)   NSA T5546BW
    BBC Radio 3, first performance 14/4/83   and BMIC

Ballad *The Bramble Briar* for guitar (1970)

    Carlos Bonell   NSA M5945BW
    BBC Radio 3, 22/10/76

    David Russell   NSA C345
    BBC Radio 3, 11/2/83   and BMIC

Ballad no I, for piano (1951)

    Composer   NSA M5616 (mono)
    BBC Home Service, 22/12/62   and BMIC

    Ronald Stevenson   NSA N5849BW
    BBC Radio 3, 25/7/76   and BMIC

Ballad no 2, for piano (1969)

    Ronald Stevenson   NSA M5849BW
    BBC Radio 3, first broadcast performance 25/7/76   and BMIC

Birthday Song for piano – 4 hands (1969)

    Geraldine and Mary Peppin   NSA M5618W (mono)
    BBC Radio 3, 7/2/68

    Isabel Beyer and Harvey Dagul   NSA T4757BW
    BBC Radio 3, 2/2/82
    British Music Information Centre, 3/3/86   BMIC

Canto di Compleanno – transcription of *Birthday Song*
by Ronald Stevenson for piano – 2 hands (1974)

    Ronald Stevenson   NSA 6243BW
    BBC Radio 3, first broadcast performance 25/9/82   and BMIC

Cello Concerto for cello and orchestra (1952)

    William Pleeth (vc) RPO/John Pritchard   NSA 2201R (mono)
    BBC Third Programme, first performance 13/5/52

    Alexander Baillie (vc) BBC Philharmonic/
    Edward Downes   NSA 8609
    BBC Radio 3, 6/12/85   and BMIC

Choriamb for orchestra (1968)

    Essex Youth Orchestra/Graham Treacher   NSA M2011R (mono)
    BBC Radio 3, first broadcast performance 26/2/70   and BMIC
    BBC Scottish SO/John Canarina. R3, 18/8/86   NSA B1148

Composers' Anthology (recording of lecture
given 12/12/68 at the British Library
National Sound Archive)   NSA T452

Concertante for two pianos – 4 hands (1982)
   Isabel Beyer and Harvey Dagul   NSA C345
   BBC Radio 3, first performance 23/4/87   and BMIC

Dance Suite for orchestra (1957)
   BBC Northern SO/George Hurst   NSA M5621W (mono)
   BBC Home Service, first performance July 1961   and BMIC

Death, be not proud, for tenor and piano (1981)
From *Four John Donne Songs*
   Kenneth Bowen (ten) Erik Levi (pf)   NSA C345
   Wigmore Hall Memorial Concert 10/7/83   and BMIC

East and West, overture for wind band (1950)
   Guildhall Symphonic Wind Band/Adrian Leaper   NSA B1028
   BBC Radio 3, 3/4/86   and BMIC

Eclogue for orchestra (1946)
   BBC Welsh Orchestra/Bryan Balkwill   NSA M5623W (moho)
   BBC Home Service, 19/1/61
   City of London Sinfonia/Richard Hickox   NSA 8166
   BBC Radio 3, 26/6/84   and BMIC

Elegiac Fugue for piano (1981)
   Composer (1981) first performance,
     Geraldine Peppin Commemoration, 1981   NSA C345
   Tape – Stevens collection   and BMIC
   James Gibb   NSA 5357BW
   BBC Radio 3, first broadcast performance 17/9/81   and BMIC

Et Resurrexit, cantata for soli, chorus and orchestra (1969)
   Sybil Michelow (contr) Philip Langridge (ten)   NSA 2178W (mono)
   Tilford Bach Festival Choir and Orchestra/   and BMIC
   Denys Darlow
   BBC Radio 3, first broadcast performance 22/1/73

Fantasia for organ (1966)

> Donald Hunt, Leeds Parish Church   NSA M1699W (mono)
> BBC Radio 3, first broadcast performance 19/6/69   and BMIC

Fantasia for two violins and piano, (1952)

> John Glickman and Sybil Copeland (vns) James
> Gibb (pf)   NSA C345
> British Music Information Centre 3/3/86   and BMIC

Fantasia on *Giles Farnaby's Dreame*, for piano (1953)

> James Gibb   NSA M5627W (mono)
> BBC Radio 3, 6/4/66   and BMIC

> Colin Horsley   NSA M5626W (mono)
> BBC Radio 3, 5/7/67

> Michael Finnissy   NSA C345
> British Music Information Centre, 3/3/86   and BMIC

Fantasia on *The Irish Ho-Hoane*, for piano – 4 hands

> Isabel Beyer and Harvey Dagul   NSA 9340BW01
> Radio 3, 26/7/85   and BMIC

Fantasia on a theme of Dowland, for violin and piano (1953)

> Ralph Holmes (vn) Wilfred Parry (pf)   NSA M5622W (mono)
> BBC Home Service, 12/7/63   and BMIC

> Madeleine Mitchell (vn) Klaus Zoll (pf)   NSA C345
> British Music Information Centre, 19/12/84   and BMIC

Five Inventions for piano (1950)

> James Gibb   NSA 991W (mono)
> BBC Music Programme, 6/4/66. Introduction by
> the composer

> James Gibb   NSA 5357BW
> BBC Radio 3, 17/9/81   and BMIC

> Marianne Eichorn   BMIC
> Stuttgart, 22/3/69
> Tape – Stevens Collection

Four John Donne Songs – see separate entries

> 1 *Sweetest love, I do not go* 2 *Go, and catch a falling star*
> 3 *The Good-morrow* 4 *Death, be not proud*

Fuga alla Sarabanda for piano (1980)

> Richard Deering   BMIC
> British Music Information Centre, first
>   performance 17/12/85
>
> Michael Finnissy   NSA C345
> British Music Information Centre, 3/3/86   and BMIC

Fugal Overture for orchestra (1947)

> BBC Scottish Orchestra/Clarence Raybould   NSA T1036W1 (Mono)
> BBC Third Programme 1956   and BMIC
> transcription of unpublished disc no. 10/420A
>
> BBC Scottish Orchestra/Stanford Robinson   NSA M5624W (Mono)
> BBC Home Service, 5/6/61   and BMIC

Go, and catch a falling star, for tenor and piano (1943)
From *Four John Donne Songs*

> René Soames (ten) composer (pf)   NSA 991W (Mono)
> BBC Home Service, 22/7/47   and BMIC
>
> Gerald English (ten) composer (pf)   NSA 991W (Mono)
> BBC Music Programme, 6/4/66   and BMIC
>
> Kenneth Bowen (ten) Paul Hamburger (pf)   NSA T5333BW
> BBC Radio 3, 8/12/82   and BMIC

The Good-morrow for tenor and piano (1943)
From *Four John Donne Songs*

> Rene Soames (ten) composer (pf)   NSA 991W (Mono)
> BBC Home Service, 22/10/47
>
> Gerald English (ten) composer (pf)   NSA 991W (Mono)
> BBC Music Programme, 6/4/66   and BMIC
>
> Kenneth Bowen (ten) Paul Hamburger (pf)   NSA T5333BW
> BBC Radio 3, 8/12/82   and BMIC
>
> Kenneth Bowen (ten) Eric Levi (pf)   NSA C345
> Wigmore Hall, Memorial Concert 10/7/83   and BHIC

Horn Trio, for horn, violin and piano (1966)

> Alan Civil (hn) Hugh Bean (vn) David Parkhouse (pf) NSA M1507R (Mono)
> BBC Radio 3, first broadcast performance 4/4/64   and BMIC

Hymn to Light, for chorus, organ, brass and percussion (1970)

> Christopher Bowers-Broadbent (org)   NSA 6234BW
> Symphoniae Sacrae Chamber Ensemble   and BMIC

BBC Singers, Richard Bradshaw (cond)
BBC Radio 3, 25/9/82

Improvisation (original version) for solo violin
Eric Gruenberg   NSA 3026
BBC Radio 3, first performance 24/5/88   and BMIC

Improvisation for solo viola (1973)
Catherine Stevens   NSA C345
Wigmore Hall, Memorial Concert 10/7/83   and BMIC
Catherine Stevens   NSA C345
British Music Information Centre, 19/12/84   and BMIC

Introduction and Allegro for two pianos – 4 hands (1957)
Geraldine and Mary Peppin   NSA T1036W2 (mono)
BBC Third Programme, first performance 30/7/58   and BMIC
transcription of unpublished disc no. 10/746A

Introduction, Variations and Fugue on a theme of
Giles Farnaby, for orchestra (1972)
Royal College of Music Chamber Orchestra/
Harvey Phillips   NSA M5615W (mono)
Concertgebouw, Amsterdam, 29/4/72   and BMIC
Bournemouth Sinfonietta/Tamas Vasary   NSA B2738
BBC Radio 3, 13/9/87   and BMIC

Lyric Suite for string trio (1958)
Madeleine Mitchell (vn) Catherine Stevens (va)
Shuna Wilson (vc)   NSA C345
British Music Information Centre, 19/12/84   and BMIC

Nocturne on a note-row of Ronald Stevenson, for piano (1979)
Ronald Stevenson   NSA 6243BW
BBC Radio 3, first broadcast performance 25/9/82 and BMIC
Ronald Stevenson   NSA C345
Wigmore Hall, Memorial Concert 10/7/83
Michael Finnissy   NSA C345
British Music Information Centre, 3/3/86   and BMIC

Piano Trio for violin, cello and piano (1942)
David Martin (vn) Florence Hooton (vc)
Geoffrey Parsons (pf)   NSA M5617W (mono)
BBC Third Programme, 7/8/60

Hugh Bean (vn) Eileen Croxford (vc) David
    Parkhouse (pf)   NSA C345
Wigmore Hall, Memorial Concert 10/7/83

same performers   NSA 9534BW
BBC Radio 3, 21/10/85   and BMIC

The Pilgrims of Hope, cantata for soli, chorus and orchestra
(revised version 1968)

Ilse Wolf (sop) John Barrow (bar)   NSA 1979W (mono)
London Bach Society Chorus, Steinitz Bach   and BMIC
    Players/Paul Steinitz
BBC Radio 3, 19/4/72

Ricercar for string orchestra (1944)

Riddick String Orchestra/Kathleen Riddick   NSA T1036W4 (mono)
BBC Home Service, 5/11/50   and BMIC
transcription of unpublished disc

The Shadow of the Glen, Opera in one act (1979)

Della Jones (m-sop) Neil Mackie (ten) John
Gibbs (bar) Paul Hudson (bass)   NSA T5591BW
Divertimenti/Howard Williams   and BMIC
BBC Radio 3, first performance 22/5/83

Sinfonietta for string orchestra (1948)

Harvey Phillips String Orchestra/Harvey Phillips   NSA M5609BW
BBC Third Programme, 30/12/58   and BMIC

Boyd Neel Orchestra/Boyd Neel   NSA M5625W (mono)
BBC Third Programme, 31/1/61

Langham Chamber Orchestra/Maurice Handford NSA B2021
BBC Radio 3, 22/4/87   and BMIC

Sonata for piano, in one movement (1954)

Clive Lythgoe   NSA T1036W3 (mono)
transcription of unpublished disc of 1954

Michael Finnissy   NSA C345
British Music Information Centre, 3/3/86   and BMIC

Sonata for violin and piano, in one movement (1940)

Max Rostal (vn) composer (pf)   NSA C345 (mono)
BBC Home Service, 22/10/47   and BMIC
transcription of unpublished disc

Henry Datyner (vn) Cherry Isherwood (pf)   NSA M226W (mono)
BBC Home Service, 1957 (?)

Clarence Myerscough (vn) composer (pf)   NSA M5620W (mono)
BBC Home Service, 22/12/62   and BMIC

Madeleine Mitchell (vn) Klaus Zoll (pf)   NSA C345
British Music Information Centre, 19/12/84   and BMIC

String Quartet no I – see 'Theme and Variations'

String Quartet no 2 (1962)

English String Quartet in *Composer's Portrait*   NSA 991W (mono)
Introduced by the composer
BBC Radio 3, 6/4/66

English String Quartet   NSA 1151W (mono)
BBC Radio 3, 24/1/68

Amphion String Quartet   NSA C345
Wigmore Hall Memorial Concert 10/7/83   and BMIC

Suite for six instruments (1967)
Flute, oboe, violin, viola da gamba (or viola), cello
    and harpsichord or piano.

Tilford Bach Festival Ensemble/Denys Darlow   NSA M1133R (mono)
BBC Radio 3, first broadcast performance 9/6/68

Same performers – BBC Radio 3, 16/3/72   NSA 3019W (mono)

RCM 20th Century Ensemble/Edwin Roxburgh   BMIC
Royal College of Music, 19/11/83

Sweetest love, I do not go, for tenor and piano (1943)
From *Four John Donne Songs*

Kenneth Bowen (ten) Paul Hamburger (pf)   NSA T5333BW
BBC Radio 3, 8/12/82   and BMIC

Symphony no 1 (*A Symphony of Liberation*), for orchestra (1945)

BBC Philharmonic Orchestra/Edward Downes   NSA B1989
BBC Radio 3, 22/6/87   and BMIC

Symphony no 2, for orchestra (1964)

BBC Northern SO/Harry Newstone   NSA 3049BW
BBC Radio 3, first performance 15/6/77

BBC Philharmonic Orchestra/Edward Downes   NSA B2887
BBC Radio 3, 16/6/88   and BMIC

Thanksgiving, motet for chorus and string orchestra (1965)

    Tilford Bach Choir and Orchestra/Denys Darlow   NSA M1805W (mono)
    BBC Radio 3, first broadcast performance 9/3/70   and BMIC

Theme and Variations for piano (1941)

    Kyla Greenbaum   NSA 7694R (mono)
    BBC Home Service, 22/10/47
    transcription of unpublished disc

    Klaus Zoll   NSA C345
    British Music Information Centre, 19/12/84   and BMIC

Theme and Variations for string quartet (1949)

    Hurwitz String Quartet   NSA 2564R (mono)
    BBC Home Service, first broadcast 13/4/50   and BMIC

    English String Quartet   NSA M5614W (mono)
    BBC Third Programme, 18/8/62

The True Dark, for baritone and piano (1974)

    Graham Titus (bar) Erik Levi (pf)   NSA 7411BW
    BBC Radio 3, first performance 26/2/78   and BMIC

    David Wilson Johnson (bar) Erik Levi (pf)   NSA C345
    Wigmore Hall Memorial Concert 10/7/83   and BMIC

The Turning World, motet for baritone, chorus and
    orchestra (1971)   NSA C345 (mono)
    Tape – Stevens collection   and BMIC

Two Dances for piano – 4 hands (1962)

    Isabel Beyer and Harvey Dagul   NSA C345 (mono)
    Purcell Room 3/2/78
    Tape – Stevens collection

Two Improvisations on folk songs for brass quintet (1954)

    Philip Jones Brass Ensemble   NSA M5628W (mono)
    BBC Home Service, first broadcast 1956
    Munich Ensemble   BMIC
    Tape – Stevens collection

Two Poetical Sketches for female chorus and string
    orchestra (1961)

    Penarth Ladies' Choir and BBC Welsh Orchestra/   NSA M1358W (mono)
    David Gruffydd Evans   and BMIC
    BBC Radio 3, first broadcast performance 5/8/68

The Upturned Glass – Film music (1947)
Titles and Suicide music   NSA C345 (mono)
London Symphony Orchestra/Muir Matheson   and BMIC
transcription from unpublished disc – Stevens
  Collection

Variations for Orchestra (1964)
BBC Northern Symphony Orchestra/   NSA 1974R (mono)
  Bryden Thomson   and BMIC
BBC Radio 3, first performance 28/4/72

Violin Concerto for violin and orchestra (1943)
Max Rostal (vn) BBC Scottish Orchestra/   NSA 2624W (mono)
Ian Whyte   and BMIC
BBC Home Service 13/3/57
Stevens collection

Raymond Cohen (vn) BBC Welsh Orchestra/
John Carewe   NSA 1520R (mono)
BBC Radio 3, 2/3/70   and BMIC

Ernst Kovacic (vn) BBC Philharmonic/   NSA C345
Edward Downes   and BMIC
BBC Studio Concert, recorded 13/12/88

Bibliography

WRITINGS BY BERNARD STEVENS (CHRONOLOGICAL)

1 The Crisis in Contemporary Art Music. Lecture given at Prague Spring Festival 1948 (MS).
2 Congress of Composers. *Philharmonic Post*, Sept/Oct: 1948 vol.IV No.7.
3 The Composer Speaks. *Our Time*, London. January 1949.
4 A Visit to the Soviet Union. *The Musical Times*, December 1952.
5 Soviet Music Today. *Anglo–Soviet Journal*, Winter 1952-3, vol.13 No.4, pp.33-5 (Written after visiting the USSR Sept. 1952 as a member of a Cultural Delegation)
6 The Composer and his Audience. *Crescendo*, 1952, No.46 pp.20-22.
7 S.S. Prokofiev. *Anglo Soviet Journal*, 1953 vol. 14 No.2.
8 An Open Letter to Shostakovitch. *The New Reasoner*, 1957 vol.1 No.1.
9 The Soviet Union. *European Music in the 20th Century*. Ed. Hartog, Routledge, Kegan and Paul, 1957.
10 Great Performances but few Creative Minds. *The News Letter*, November 1957 vol.1 No.27.
11 The Music of the Soviet Union. *Guide to Modern Music on Records*, Ed. Simpson 1958. Anthony Blond.
12 Rutland Boughton. *The New Reasoner*, Spring 1959, No.8, pp.74-81.
13 Shostakovitch and the British Composer in *Shostakovitch: the Man and his Music*, Ed. Christopher Norris. Lawrence and Wishart, 1959.
14 Shostakovitch Masterpieces. Record Reviews of Fifth and Tenth Symphonies and Piano Quintet. *Anglo-Soviet Journal* 1960, vol.21 No.3.
15 Rubbra at Seventy. *Royal College of Music Magazine* 1971, vol.67 No.3.
16 The Symphonies of Shostakovitch. Purcell Room, Southbank, Lecture 6.11.72 (MS).
   Report by Frank Stokes, on Purcell Room Lecture given 6.11.72. *Music and Life*, London, No.46, January 1973.
17 Report by Frank Stokes, on Lecture 'Shostakovitch – an assessment of his achievement' given Marx House 12.10.75. in *Music and Life*, London No.52, February 1975.

18 Composers' Anthology No.6 – Lecture given December 1968 at British National Sound Archive. Printed in *Recorded Sound Journal* of BNSA October 1975 No.60, pp.477-485.

19 Shostakovitch: His Music. *Artery* – A Cultural Journal of Left Unity. Winter 1975.

20 Profile: Dr. Bernard Stevens in Conversation with Wally Ward. *Workers' Music Association Bulletin*, October 1978, No.7: excerpts reprinted in *WMA Bulletin (Bernard Stevens Memorial issue)* October 1983, No.4.

21 Alan Bush, 'The Choral Music and Personal Recollections' in *An 80th Birthday Symposium* Edited, Ronald Stevenson. Bravura Publications 1981.

22 Alan Rawsthorne, vol 2. Personal Recollections. Bravura Publications 1984.

23 Alan Rawsthorne, vol 3. The Choral Music. Bravura Publications 1986.

WRITINGS ABOUT BERNARD STEVENS (ALPHABETICAL BY AUTHOR)

Barrell, Bernard. East Anglian Report. *Composer*, Spring 1983.

Bush, Alan, Contribution to *WMA Bulletin*, (Bernard Stevens Memorial Issue) October 1983, No.4.

Bushby, Elizabeth. Musical Partnership. *Essex County Standard* (Magazine Section) 17.11.1967.

Cooke, Richard. 'Stevens, Bernard'. *The New Grove Dictionary of Music and Musicians'*, Vol.18 pp.132-133. London 1980.

Cruft, Adrian. Bernard Stevens. *Royal College of Music Magazine* 1983 Vol.79 No 2.

Daily Express, 29.3.46. £250 Symphony written in the Blitz.

Day, Francis. Reminiscences in *WMA Bulletin*, (Bernard Stevens Memorial Issue) October 1983, No.4.

Horrocks, Joan. Memories of Bernard Stevens, *WMA Bulletin*, (Bernard Stevens Memorial Issue) October 1983, No.4.

Horowitz, Joseph. Reviews of Two Improvisations for Brass Quintet and Four John Donne Songs. *Royal College of Music Magazine* vol.82 No.1.

H.G.A. Two Prize-Winning Symphonies. *Manchester Guardian* 17.6.1946.

Keller, Hans. Theme and Variations for String Quartet Op.II. Review and Analysis, *Music Review*, 1952 vol.13, p.243.

London Philharmonic Post, Composer of Today March 1947, Vol.3 No.10.

Mason, Colin. The Music of Bernard Stevens. *The Listener*, 12.3.1959, p.487.

Miller, John. Recollections. *WMA Bulletin*, (Bernard Stevens Memorial Issue) October 1983, No.4.

MacDonald, Calum. Lost Generation. *The Listener*, 23.4.1987, p.32.

MacDonald, Calum. Bernard Stevens's Violin Concerto. *Music and Musicians*, December 1988.

Robinson, Sean. The Music Lovers. *Halstead Advertiser*, January 1974.

Rubbra, Edmund. Bernard Stevens. *Royal College of Music Magazine*, 1983 vol.78, No.2.

Sear, H.G. Dedicated to Clive Branson. *Daily Worker*, June 1946.

Stainer, John. Bernard Stevens. *Royal College of Music Magazine*, 1983 vol.79 No.3.

Stevenson, Ronald. Bernard Stevens. *The Musical Times*, June 1968 No.1504 vol.109 pp.525-527.

Stevenson, Ronald. Bernard Stevens 1916-1983, *Tempo*, 1983 No. 145. p.27.

Swanston, Roderick. Bernard Stevens Suite for Six Instruments. Programme exposé, Royal College of Music. 1983.

The Musical Times, Bernard Stevens, March 1983, p.186.

The Times, Dr. Bernard Stevens, 8.1.83.

Trowell, Brian. Report of Bernard Stevens Memorial Concert, Wigmore Hall, July 10th 1983. *The Musical Times*, September 1983.

Author Unknown. Composer of Today. *London Philharmonic Post*, March 1947, vol.III No.10.

Catalogue of Works

28	Dance Suite for orchestra (1957)	Lengnick
29	Introduction and Allegro for two pianos (1957)	MS
30	*Lyric Suite* for string trio (1958)	Bardic
31a*	Adagio and Fugue for wind band (1959)	Bardic
31b*	Prelude and Finale for orchestra (1960)	Novello
32	*Two Poetical Sketches* (William Blake) for women's voices and strings or piano (1961)	Bardic
33	Two Dances for piano duet (1962)	Roberton
34	String Quartet no 2 (1962)	Stainer and Bell
35	Symphony No 2 (1964)	MS
36	Variations for Orchestra (1964)	MS
37	*Thanksgiving* (Tagore) Motet for SATB chorus and string orchestra or organ (1965)	MS
38	Trio for horn, violin and piano (1966)	MS
39	Fantasia for organ (1966)	Bardic
40	Suite for Six Instruments (1967) violin, oboe, flute, viola da gamba or viola, cello, harpsichord or piano	MS
41	*Choriamb* for orchestra (1968)	Novello
42	Ballad No 2 for Piano (1969)	Roberton
43	*Et Resurrexit* (Ecclesiastes and Randall Swingler) Cantata for alto and tenor soloists, chorus and orchestra (1969)	MS
44	*Hymn to Light* (Tagore) Anthem for chorus, organ, brass and percussion	Roberton
45	*The Bramble Briar*. Ballad for guitar (1910)	Bèrben
46	*The Turning World* (Randall Swingler) Motet for baritone solo, chorus, orchestra and piano (1971)	MS
47	Introduction, Variations and Fugue on a theme of Giles Farnaby, for orchestra (1972)	Lengnick
48	Improvisation for solo violin	Roberton
	Improvisation for solo viola (1973)	Roberton
49	*The True Dark* (Randall Swingler). Song-cycle for baritone and piano (1974)	Roberton
50	*The Shadow of the Glen* (J.M. Synge), an Opera in one act (1978/9) Mezzo soprano, tenor, baritone and bass soloists, chamber orchestra.	MS
51	Nocturne – on a note-row of Ronald Stevenson, for piano (1979)	Roberton
52	*Autumn Sequence* for guitar and harpsichord (1980)	Bèrben
53*	*Death be not Proud* (John Donne) for high voice and piano (1981) published with Opus 5 without opus no.	Stainer and Bell
54*	Concerto for piano and orchestra (1981) (revised version of Op 26)	MS
55*	Concertante for two pianos (1982)	MS

1936	Toccata and Fugue for piano	Bardic
1937	Four Canons for two oboes and bassoon	Bardic
1937?	Invention for Piano	Bardic
1937	*Two Beddoes Songs* (Beddoes) for tenor and piano	Bardic
1937?	Two Chorale Preludes for organ	Bardic
1938?	Mass for unaccompanied double choir	MS
1943	*One Day* (David Martin) SATB chorus and piano	WMA
1947?	*Song of the Waking World* (Randall Swingler) in *The WMA Anniversary Song Book*. Unison song.	WMA
1947	*Colliers' Song* (Kathleen Nott) for male voices and piano.	WMA
1947	*If we die* (Ethel Rosenberg) for high voice and piano	MS
1947	Three Pieces from *The Upturned Glass* for piano	Bardic
1951	*Take all of Man* (Randall Swingler). An ode for mixed choir unaccompanied	MS
1952	Piano Pieces (9) contributed to *Five by Ten* (Five Piano Albums for Study and Recreation) also published separately	Lengnick
1962	*Aria* for piano	Roberton
1963	*Birthday Song* for piano duet	Stainer and Bell
1968	*Running to Paradise* (W.B. Yeats) SATB chorus and piano.	Novello
1974	*Canto di Compleanno*	Roberton
	(*Birthday Song* transcribed for solo piano by Ronald Stevenson)	
1974?	Fughetta for organ on one manual	Bardic
1980	*Elegiac Fugue* on the name 'Geraldine', for piano	Roberton
1980	*Fuga alla Sarabanda* for piano	Roberton

Film Music

1947	The Upturned Glass	MS
1947	The Mark of Cain	MS
1948	Once a Jolly Swagman	MS

Works marked MS are unpublished but material is obtainable. Details from British Music Information Centre, 10 Stratford Place. London W1.
★ = Opus number added posthumously.
Information in Discography, Bibliography and Catalogue of Works is correct as at 31.3.1989.
Bernard Stevens original manuscrips are now in The British Library as Additional Manuscripts 68944-69035.

Index

REFERENCES TO SPECIFIC WORKS BY BERNARD STEVENS: